The National Parks of England and Wales

The National Parks of England and Wales

TOGETHER WITH AREAS OF OUTSTANDING NATURAL BEAUTY AND LONG-DISTANCE FOOTPATHS AND BRIDLEWAYS

by

ROGER BUSH

4 colour plates and 128 monochrome photographs, 8 maps

J. M. DENT & SONS LTD

LONDON

ISBN 0 460 07849 6

Contents

Illustrations

Maps, pages 11 to 18

COLOUR PLATES

BLACK-AND-WHITE ILLUSTRATIONS

National Parks

8

Long-Distance Footpaths and Bridleways

Author's Note

Many people have helped with the preparation of this book through written or verbal contributions, but individual sections have not been checked locally and I must therefore take responsibility for any factual errors. The national park information officers have been unfailingly helpful, and, among colleagues at the Countryside Commission, Paul Gilling, who drew the maps, and Joyce Foster, who helped with the collection and choice of illustrations, must especially be mentioned.

R.B.

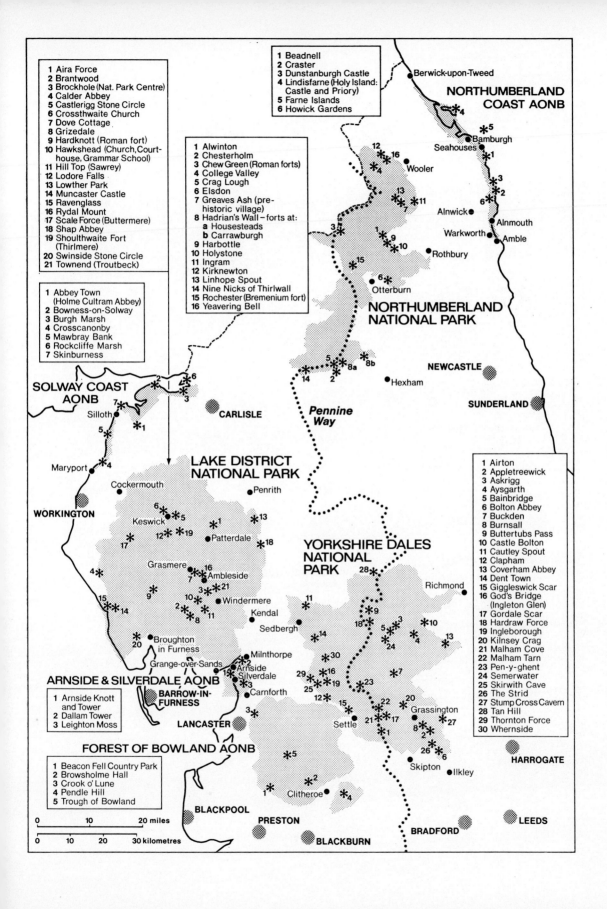

Lake District legend:

1 Aira Force
2 Brantwood
3 Brockhole (Nat. Park Centre)
4 Calder Abbey
5 Castlerigg Stone Circle
6 Crossthwaite Church
7 Dove Cottage
8 Grizedale
9 Hardknott (Roman fort)
10 Hawkshead (Church, Court-house, Grammar School)
11 Hill Top (Sawrey)
12 Lodore Falls
13 Lowther Park
14 Muncaster Castle
15 Ravenglass
16 Rydal Mount
17 Scale Force (Buttermere)
18 Shap Abbey
19 Shoulthwaite Fort (Thirlmere)
20 Swinside Stone Circle
21 Townend (Troutbeck)

Solway Coast legend:

1 Abbey Town (Holme Cultram Abbey)
2 Bowness-on-Solway
3 Burgh Marsh
4 Crosscanonby
5 Mawbray Bank
6 Rockcliffe Marsh
7 Skinburness

Northumberland Coast legend:

1 Beadnell
2 Craster
3 Dunstanburgh Castle
4 Lindisfarne (Holy Island: Castle and Priory)
5 Farne Islands
6 Howick Gardens

Northumberland National Park legend:

1 Alwinton
2 Chesterholm
3 Chew Green (Roman forts)
4 College Valley
5 Crag Lough
6 Elsdon
7 Greaves Ash (prehistoric village)
8 Hadrian's Wall – forts at:
  a Housesteads
  b Carrawburgh
9 Harbottle
10 Holystone
11 Ingram
12 Kirknewton
13 Linhope Spout
14 Nine Nicks of Thirlwall
15 Rochester (Bremenium fort)
16 Yeavering Bell

Yorkshire Dales legend:

1 Airton
2 Appletreewick
3 Askrigg
4 Aysgarth
5 Bainbridge
6 Bolton Abbey
7 Buckden
8 Burnsall
9 Buttertubs Pass
10 Castle Bolton
11 Cautley Spout
12 Clapham
13 Coverham Abbey
14 Dent Town
15 Giggleswick Scar
16 God's Bridge (Ingleton Glen)
17 Gordale Scar
18 Hardraw Force
19 Ingleborough
20 Kilnsey Crag
21 Malham Cove
22 Malham Tarn
23 Pen-y-ghent
24 Semerwater
25 Skirwith Cave
26 The Strid
27 Stump Cross Cavern
28 Tan Hill
29 Thornton Force
30 Whernside

Arnside & Silverdale legend:

1 Arnside Knott and Tower
2 Dallam Tower
3 Leighton Moss

Forest of Bowland legend:

1 Beacon Fell Country Park
2 Browsholme Hall
3 Crook o' Lune
4 Pendle Hill
5 Trough of Bowland

NORTHUMBERLAND COAST AONB
Berwick-upon-Tweed
Bamburgh
Seahouses
Wooler
Alnwick
Alnmouth
Warkworth
Amble
Rothbury
NORTHUMBERLAND NATIONAL PARK
Otterburn
NEWCASTLE
Hexham
SUNDERLAND
Pennine Way

SOLWAY COAST AONB
Silloth
Maryport
CARLISLE
WORKINGTON
Cockermouth
Penrith
Keswick
LAKE DISTRICT NATIONAL PARK
Patterdale
Grasmere
Ambleside
Windermere
Kendal
Sedbergh
Broughton in Furness
Milnthorpe
Grange-over-Sands
Arnside
Silverdale
Carnforth
ARNSIDE & SILVERDALE AONB
BARROW-IN-FURNESS
LANCASTER
FOREST OF BOWLAND AONB
Clitheroe
BLACKPOOL
PRESTON
BLACKBURN

YORKSHIRE DALES NATIONAL PARK
Richmond
Settle
Grassington
Skipton
Ilkley
HARROGATE
BRADFORD
LEEDS

0   10   20 miles
0   10   20   30 kilometres

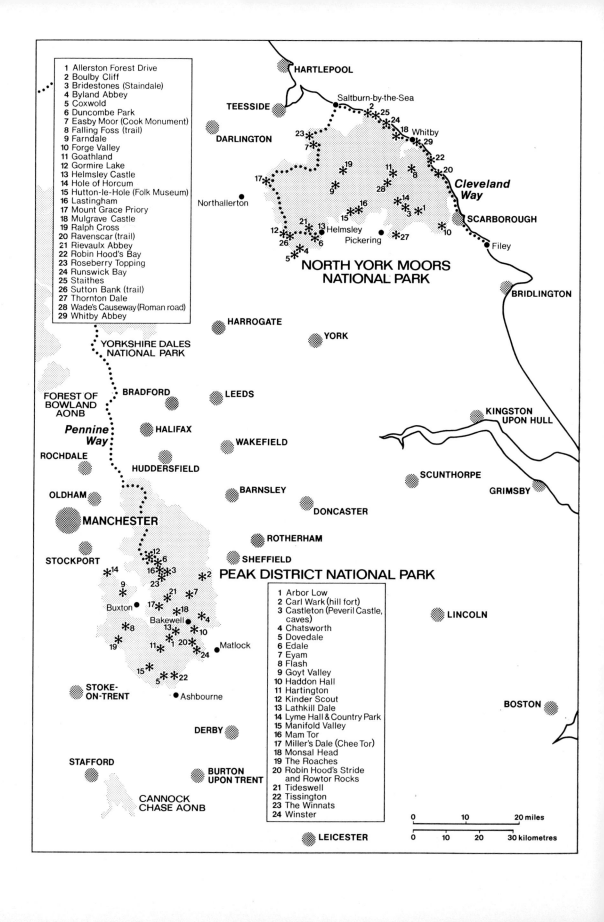

1 Allerston Forest Drive
2 Boulby Cliff
3 Bridestones (Staindale)
4 Byland Abbey
5 Coxwold
6 Duncombe Park
7 Easby Moor (Cook Monument)
8 Falling Foss (trail)
9 Farndale
10 Forge Valley
11 Goathland
12 Gormire Lake
13 Helmsley Castle
14 Hole of Horcum
15 Hutton-le-Hole (Folk Museum)
16 Lastingham
17 Mount Grace Priory
18 Mulgrave Castle
19 Ralph Cross
20 Ravenscar (trail)
21 Rievaulx Abbey
22 Robin Hood's Bay
23 Roseberry Topping
24 Runswick Bay
25 Staithes
26 Sutton Bank (trail)
27 Thornton Dale
28 Wade's Causeway (Roman road)
29 Whitby Abbey

HARTLEPOOL
Saltburn-by-the-Sea
TEESSIDE
DARLINGTON
Northallerton
Whitby
Cleveland Way
SCARBOROUGH
Helmsley
Pickering
Filey
NORTH YORK MOORS NATIONAL PARK
BRIDLINGTON

HARROGATE
YORK

YORKSHIRE DALES NATIONAL PARK

FOREST OF BOWLAND AONB
BRADFORD
LEEDS
KINGSTON UPON HULL
Pennine Way
HALIFAX
WAKEFIELD
ROCHDALE
HUDDERSFIELD
SCUNTHORPE
GRIMSBY
OLDHAM
BARNSLEY
MANCHESTER
DONCASTER
STOCKPORT
ROTHERHAM
SHEFFIELD
PEAK DISTRICT NATIONAL PARK
Buxton
Bakewell
Matlock
LINCOLN

1 Arbor Low
2 Carl Wark (hill fort)
3 Castleton (Peveril Castle, caves)
4 Chatsworth
5 Dovedale
6 Edale
7 Eyam
8 Flash
9 Goyt Valley
10 Haddon Hall
11 Hartington
12 Kinder Scout
13 Lathkill Dale
14 Lyme Hall & Country Park
15 Manifold Valley
16 Mam Tor
17 Miller's Dale (Chee Tor)
18 Monsal Head
19 The Roaches
20 Robin Hood's Stride and Rowtor Rocks
21 Tideswell
22 Tissington
23 The Winnats
24 Winster

STOKE-ON-TRENT
Ashbourne
BOSTON
STAFFORD
DERBY
BURTON UPON TRENT
CANNOCK CHASE AONB

0   10   20 miles
0 10 20 30 kilometres

LEICESTER

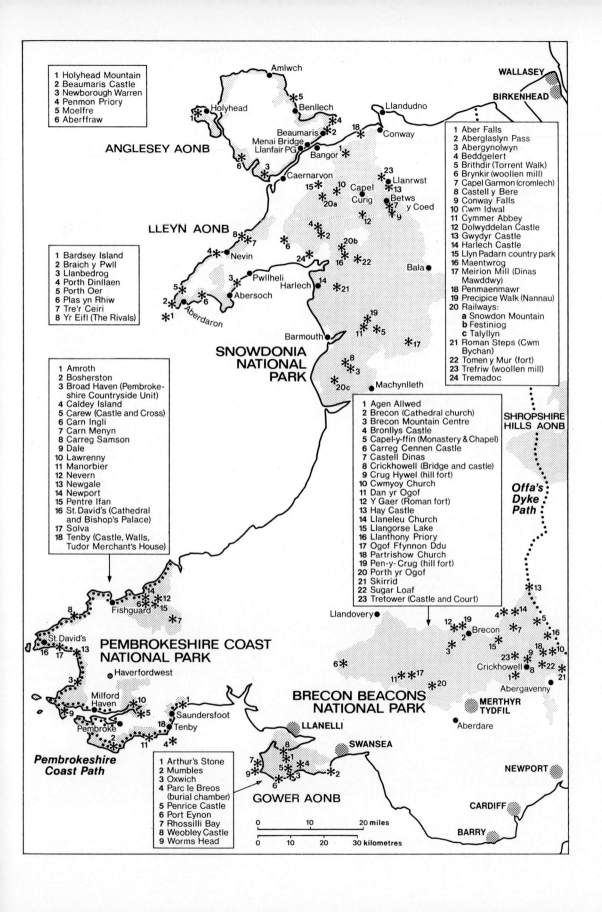

WALLASEY

BIRKENHEAD

Amlwch

Holyhead

Benllech

ANGLESEY AONB

Beaumaris

Menai Bridge

Llanfair PG

Bangor

Caernarvon

LLEYN AONB

Nevin

Pwllheli

Abersoch

Aberdaron

Harlech

SNOWDONIA NATIONAL PARK

Barmouth

Machynlleth

Bala

Llandudno

Conway

Llanrwst

Capel Curig

Betws y Coed

1 Holyhead Mountain
2 Beaumaris Castle
3 Newborough Warren
4 Penmon Priory
5 Moelfre
6 Aberffraw

1 Bardsey Island
2 Braich y Pwll
3 Llanbedrog
4 Porth Dinllaen
5 Porth Oer
6 Plas yn Rhiw
7 Tre'r Ceiri
8 Yr Eifl (The Rivals)

1 Aber Falls
2 Aberglaslyn Pass
3 Abergynolwyn
4 Beddgelert
5 Brithdir (Torrent Walk)
6 Brynkir (woollen mill)
7 Capel Garmon (cromlech)
8 Castell y Bere
9 Conway Falls
10 Cwm Idwal
11 Cymmer Abbey
12 Dolwyddelan Castle
13 Gwydyr Castle
14 Harlech Castle
15 Llyn Padarn country park
16 Maentwrog
17 Meirion Mill (Dinas Mawddwy)
18 Penmaenmawr
19 Precipice Walk (Nannau)
20 Railways:
 a Snowdon Mountain
 b Festiniog
 c Talyllyn
21 Roman Steps (Cwm Bychan)
22 Tomen y Mur (fort)
23 Trefriw (woollen mill)
24 Tremadoc

1 Amroth
2 Bosherston
3 Broad Haven (Pembroke-shire Countryside Unit)
4 Caldey Island
5 Carew (Castle and Cross)
6 Carn Ingli
7 Carn Menyn
8 Carreg Samson
9 Dale
10 Lawrenny
11 Manorbier
12 Nevern
13 Newgale
14 Newport
15 Pentre Ifan
16 St. David's (Cathedral and Bishop's Palace)
17 Solva
18 Tenby (Castle, Walls, Tudor Merchant's House)

SHROPSHIRE HILLS AONB

Offa's Dyke Path

1 Agen Allwed
2 Brecon (Cathedral church)
3 Brecon Mountain Centre
4 Bronllys Castle
5 Capel-y-ffin (Monastery & Chapel)
6 Carreg Cennen Castle
7 Castell Dinas
8 Crickhowell (Bridge and castle)
9 Crug Hywel (hill fort)
10 Cwmyoy Church
11 Dan yr Ogof
12 Y Gaer (Roman fort)
13 Hay Castle
14 Llaneleu Church
15 Llangorse Lake
16 Llanthony Priory
17 Ogof Ffynnon Ddu
18 Partrishow Church
19 Pen-y-Crug (hill fort)
20 Porth yr Ogof
21 Skirrid
22 Sugar Loaf
23 Tretower (Castle and Court)

Llandovery

Fishguard

St. David's

Haverfordwest

Milford Haven

Pembroke

Saundersfoot

Tenby

PEMBROKESHIRE COAST NATIONAL PARK

Pembrokeshire Coast Path

BRECON BEACONS NATIONAL PARK

Brecon

Crickhowell

Abergavenny

MERTHYR TYDFIL

Aberdare

LLANELLI

SWANSEA

NEWPORT

CARDIFF

BARRY

1 Arthur's Stone
2 Mumbles
3 Oxwich
4 Parc le Breos (burial chamber)
5 Penrice Castle
6 Port Eynon
7 Rhossilli Bay
8 Weobley Castle
9 Worms Head

GOWER AONB

0   10   20 miles

0 10   20   30 kilometres

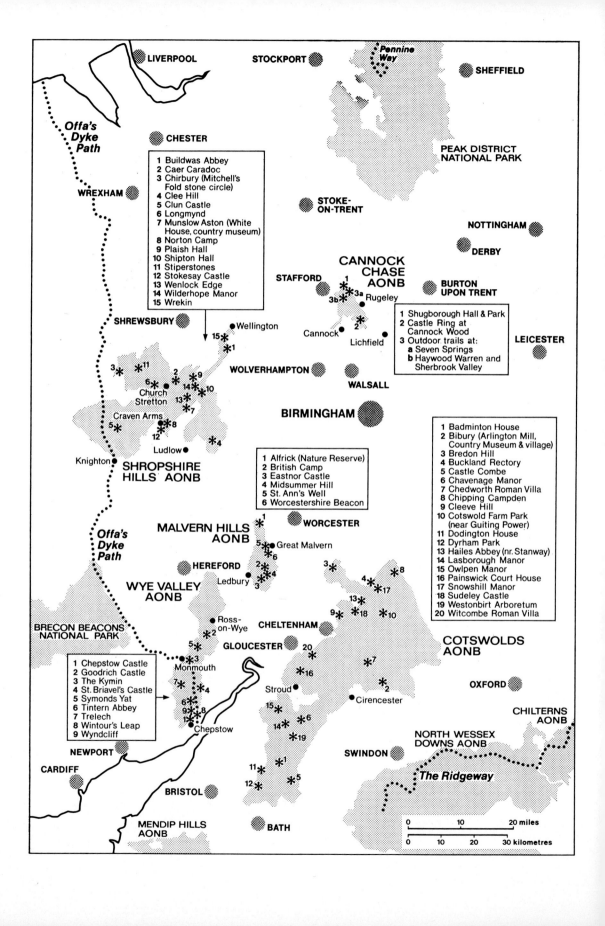

Offa's Dyke Path

LIVERPOOL

STOCKPORT

Pennine Way

SHEFFIELD

CHESTER

PEAK DISTRICT NATIONAL PARK

WREXHAM

1 Buildwas Abbey
2 Caer Caradoc
3 Chirbury (Mitchell's Fold stone circle)
4 Clee Hill
5 Clun Castle
6 Longmynd
7 Munslow Aston (White House, country museum)
8 Norton Camp
9 Plaish Hall
10 Shipton Hall
11 Stiperstones
12 Stokesay Castle
13 Wenlock Edge
14 Wilderhope Manor
15 Wrekin

STOKE-ON-TRENT

NOTTINGHAM

DERBY

CANNOCK CHASE AONB

STAFFORD

BURTON UPON TRENT

Rugeley

SHREWSBURY

Wellington

Cannock

Lichfield

LEICESTER

1 Shugborough Hall & Park
2 Castle Ring at Cannock Wood
3 Outdoor trails at:
  a Seven Springs
  b Haywood Warren and Sherbrook Valley

WOLVERHAMPTON

Church Stretton

WALSALL

Craven Arms

BIRMINGHAM

Ludlow

Knighton

SHROPSHIRE HILLS AONB

1 Alfrick (Nature Reserve)
2 British Camp
3 Eastnor Castle
4 Midsummer Hill
5 St. Ann's Well
6 Worcestershire Beacon

WORCESTER

1 Badminton House
2 Bibury (Arlington Mill, Country Museum & village)
3 Bredon Hill
4 Buckland Rectory
5 Castle Combe
6 Chavenage Manor
7 Chedworth Roman Villa
8 Chipping Campden
9 Cleeve Hill
10 Cotswold Farm Park (near Guiting Power)
11 Dodington House
12 Dyrham Park
13 Hailes Abbey (nr. Stanway)
14 Lasborough Manor
15 Owlpen Manor
16 Painswick Court House
17 Snowshill Manor
18 Sudeley Castle
19 Westonbirt Arboretum
20 Witcombe Roman Villa

MALVERN HILLS AONB

Great Malvern

HEREFORD

WYE VALLEY AONB

Ledbury

Offa's Dyke Path

BRECON BEACONS NATIONAL PARK

Ross-on-Wye

CHELTENHAM

GLOUCESTER

COTSWOLDS AONB

1 Chepstow Castle
2 Goodrich Castle
3 The Kymin
4 St. Briavel's Castle
5 Symonds Yat
6 Tintern Abbey
7 Trelech
8 Wintour's Leap
9 Wyndcliff

Monmouth

Stroud

Cirencester

OXFORD

NEWPORT

Chepstow

CHILTERNS AONB

CARDIFF

NORTH WESSEX DOWNS AONB

SWINDON

BRISTOL

The Ridgeway

MENDIP HILLS AONB

BATH

0   10   20 miles

0   10   20   30 kilometres

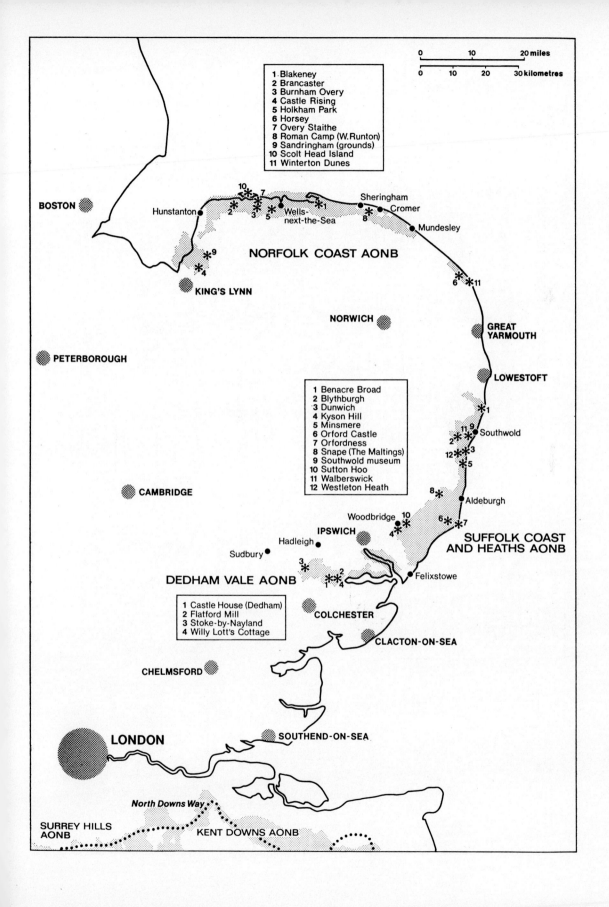

1 Blakeney
2 Brancaster
3 Burnham Overy
4 Castle Rising
5 Holkham Park
6 Horsey
7 Overy Staithe
8 Roman Camp (W. Runton)
9 Sandringham (grounds)
10 Scolt Head Island
11 Winterton Dunes

0   10   20 miles
0   10   20   30 kilometres

BOSTON

Hunstanton   Wells-next-the-Sea   Sheringham   Cromer   Mundesley

NORFOLK COAST AONB

KING'S LYNN

NORWICH

PETERBOROUGH

GREAT YARMOUTH

LOWESTOFT

1 Benacre Broad
2 Blythburgh
3 Dunwich
4 Kyson Hill
5 Minsmere
6 Orford Castle
7 Orfordness
8 Snape (The Maltings)
9 Southwold museum
10 Sutton Hoo
11 Walberswick
12 Westleton Heath

Southwold

CAMBRIDGE

Aldeburgh

Woodbridge   IPSWICH

Hadleigh

Sudbury

SUFFOLK COAST
AND HEATHS AONB

DEDHAM VALE AONB

Felixstowe

1 Castle House (Dedham)
2 Flatford Mill
3 Stoke-by-Nayland
4 Willy Lott's Cottage

COLCHESTER

CLACTON-ON-SEA

CHELMSFORD

LONDON

SOUTHEND-ON-SEA

North Downs Way

SURREY HILLS
AONB

KENT DOWNS AONB

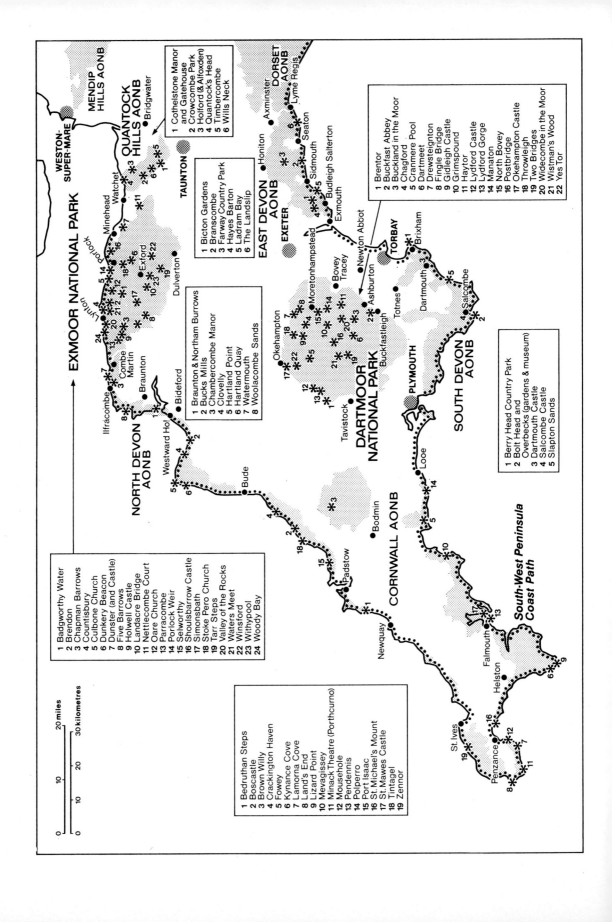

South-West Peninsula Coast Path

EXMOOR NATIONAL PARK

1 Badworthy Water
2 Brendon
3 Chapman Barrows
4 Countisbury
5 Culbone Church
6 Dunkery Beacon
7 Dunster (and Castle)
8 Five Barrows
9 Holwell Castle
10 Landacre Bridge
11 Nettlecombe Court
12 Oare Church
13 Parracombe
14 Porlock Weir
15 Selworthy
16 Shoulsbarrow Castle
17 Simonsbath
18 Stoke Pero Church
19 Tarr Steps
20 Valley of the Rocks
21 Waters Meet
22 Winsford
23 Withypool
24 Woody Bay

QUANTOCK HILLS AONB

1 Cothelstone Manor and Gatehouse
2 Crowcombe Park
3 Holford (& Alfoxden)
4 Quantock's Head
5 Timbercombe
6 Wills Neck

EAST DEVON AONB

1 Bicton Gardens
2 Branscombe
3 Farway Country Park
4 Hayes Barton
5 Ladram Bay
6 The Landslip

DARTMOOR NATIONAL PARK

1 Brentor
2 Buckfast Abbey
3 Buckland in the Moor
4 Chagford
5 Cranmere Pool
6 Dartmeet
7 Drewsteignton
8 Fingle Bridge
9 Gidleigh Castle
10 Grimspound
11 Haytor
12 Lydford Castle
13 Lydford Gorge
14 Manaton
15 North Bovey
16 Postbridge
17 Okehampton Castle
18 Throwleigh
19 Two Bridges
20 Widecombe in the Moor
21 Wistman's Wood
22 Yes Tor

NORTH DEVON AONB

1 Braunton & Northam Burrows
2 Bucks Mills
3 Chambercombe Manor
4 Clovelly
5 Hartland Point
6 Hartland Quay
7 Watermouth
8 Woolacombe Sands

SOUTH DEVON AONB

1 Berry Head Country Park
2 Bolt Head and Overbecks (gardens & museum)
3 Dartmouth Castle
4 Salcombe Castle
5 Slapton Sands

CORNWALL AONB

1 Bedruthan Steps
2 Boscastle
3 Brown Willy
4 Crackington Haven
5 Fowey
6 Kynance Cove
7 Lamorna Cove
8 Land's End
9 Lizard Point
10 Mevagissey
11 Minack Theatre (Porthcurno)
12 Mousehole
13 Pendennis
14 Polperro
15 Port Isaac
16 St. Michael's Mount
17 St. Mawes Castle
18 Tintagel
19 Zennor

MENDIP HILLS AONB

DORSET AONB

WESTON-SUPER-MARE

TAUNTON

EXETER

TORBAY

PLYMOUTH

Minehead
Watchet
Bridgwater
Axminster
Lyme Regis
Seaton
Honiton
Sidmouth
Budleigh Salterton
Exmouth
Newton Abbot
Brixham
Dartmouth
Salcombe
Totnes
Ashburton
Buckfastleigh
Bovey Tracey
Moretonhampstead
Okehampton
Tavistock
Looe
Bodmin
Bude
Bideford
Braunton
Ilfracombe
Westward Ho!
Newquay
Padstow
St Ives
Penzance
Helston
Falmouth

Lynton
Combe Martin
Dulverton
Exford

20 miles

30 kilometres

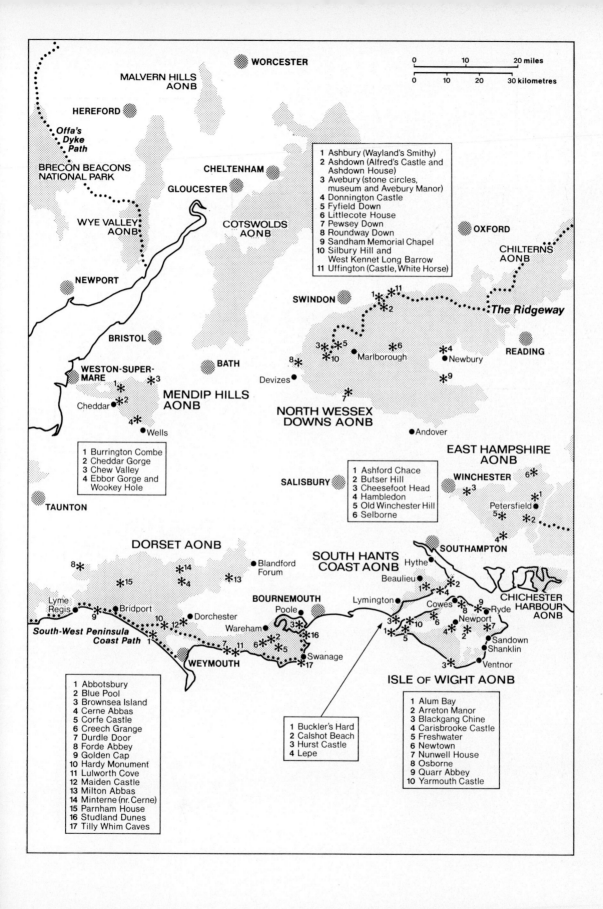

WORCESTER

MALVERN HILLS
AONB

HEREFORD

*Offa's
Dyke
Path*

BRECON BEACONS
NATIONAL PARK

CHELTENHAM

GLOUCESTER

WYE VALLEY
AONB

COTSWOLDS
AONB

OXFORD

NEWPORT

CHILTERNS
AONB

1 Ashbury (Wayland's Smithy)
2 Ashdown (Alfred's Castle and
   Ashdown House)
3 Avebury (stone circles,
   museum and Avebury Manor)
4 Donnington Castle
5 Fyfield Down
6 Littlecote House
7 Pewsey Down
8 Roundway Down
9 Sandham Memorial Chapel
10 Silbury Hill and
    West Kennet Long Barrow
11 Uffington (Castle, White Horse)

SWINDON

The Ridgeway

BRISTOL

BATH

READING

WESTON-SUPER-
MARE

Cheddar

Marlborough

Newbury

MENDIP HILLS
AONB

Devizes

Wells

NORTH WESSEX
DOWNS AONB

Andover

EAST HAMPSHIRE
AONB

WINCHESTER

1 Burrington Combe
2 Cheddar Gorge
3 Chew Valley
4 Ebbor Gorge and
   Wookey Hole

SALISBURY

Petersfield

TAUNTON

1 Ashford Chace
2 Butser Hill
3 Cheesefoot Head
4 Hambledon
5 Old Winchester Hill
6 Selborne

DORSET AONB

Blandford
Forum

SOUTH HANTS
COAST AONB

Hythe

SOUTHAMPTON

Beaulieu

CHICHESTER
HARBOUR
AONB

Lyme
Regis

Bridport

Lymington

Cowes

Ryde

*South-West Peninsula
Coast Path*

Dorchester

BOURNEMOUTH

Poole

Newport

Wareham

Sandown
Shanklin

WEYMOUTH

Swanage

Ventnor

ISLE OF WIGHT AONB

1 Abbotsbury
2 Blue Pool
3 Brownsea Island
4 Cerne Abbas
5 Corfe Castle
6 Creech Grange
7 Durdle Door
8 Forde Abbey
9 Golden Cap
10 Hardy Monument
11 Lulworth Cove
12 Maiden Castle
13 Milton Abbas
14 Minterne (nr. Cerne)
15 Parnham House
16 Studland Dunes
17 Tilly Whim Caves

1 Buckler's Hard
2 Calshot Beach
3 Hurst Castle
4 Lepe

1 Alum Bay
2 Arreton Manor
3 Blackgang Chine
4 Carisbrooke Castle
5 Freshwater
6 Newtown
7 Nunwell House
8 Osborne
9 Quarr Abbey
10 Yarmouth Castle

0   10   20 miles
0   10   20   30 kilometres

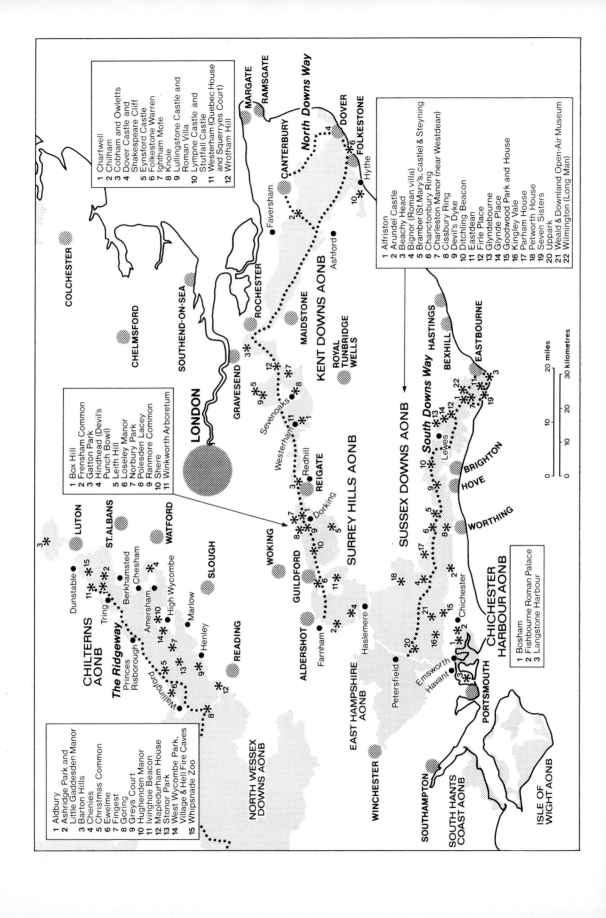

Introduction

———— ◁ ▷ ————

Nearly seventeen per cent of the countryside of England and Wales is today designated as national park or area of outstanding natural beauty. Yet these terms remain a puzzle to many people, who cannot see why a national park cannot be nationally owned, or at any rate be a 'park', and are curious as to how natural beauty is assessed to be outstanding. It is far from easy to understand what is meant without relating the terms to the way in which we now control the development of the land in which we live.

Nowadays everybody accepts that one cannot, simply by virtue of owning a piece of land, build whatever one likes on it. Plans for any project, whether it is a bungalow or a steelworks, must be laid at the appropriate office, that of the local planning authority. It is a surprise to find that this control of land users' individual plans, so as to fit them into a coherent pattern, has such recent origins; town and country planning did not enter the statute book until 1925. And the first national park was not designated until 1950.

Designation is intimately linked with the planning process, for the parks are really a way of planning land use over a certain chosen area. First there is the decision that the area has a quality which, in considering future change and development, will be protected wherever possible. Second, there is the recognition that this protection has meaning only if people are enabled to get the benefit of the beauty and quietness that unspoilt country can offer. In a country where four-fifths of the population live in urban areas it can quickly be seen that the running of a national park calls for considerable skills of planning and management.

There has been criticism of national parks in recent years. Some critics have complained that their defences of development control are quite inadequate against large and powerful enterprises, others that the provision of facilities for visitors to the park has been too slow, or that public access to open country is still too restricted. Yet despite some of the disadvantages arising from the compromise solutions of the National Parks Act, the parks have achieved a good deal. Anyone who remembers the rash of speculative building that defaced some of our finest countryside in the between-war years can easily imagine what might have happened by now around the head of Windermere in the Lake District, or on the Pembrokeshire Coast, or in the Sheffield and Manchester commuter belts of the Peak District. And the millions who have benefited from the advice and guidance of the park warden services, planned their holiday time with the help of the information centres, or discovered car parking and public lavatories in country areas where the rate would hardly raise the cost of an earth closet, will certainly have a better idea of the positive side of park planning.

Something of the qualities for which so large a proportion of our countryside has been chosen and designated can be gleaned from the admittedly brief descriptions of the ten parks and thirty areas of outstanding natural beauty which follow. The nature of the landscape is perhaps more easily appreciated from the pictures, but some understanding of what lies under it can help enormously. The pattern of hill and valley becomes clearer, the colour of the soil straight away means something and the local building stones are more than just quaint. Many of the areas are uplands where the geology is 'solid' and the landform is well related to the structure.

On any travels through the countryside two entertaining commentators, Defoe and Cobbett, writing just a century apart, are good companions. Quite often they throw light on aspects of today's scene which are hard to explain. Both had sharp observations to make on the economy of the regions through which they journeyed, Defoe throughout the land and Cobbett mainly in the south. And to appreciate the forces which have shaped the British countryside one needs to be a time traveller as well.

In these thumbnail sketches I have also tried to indicate some of the features which make each area interesting to the visitor. The lists of places of interest are necessarily arbitrary, but they include villages, churches, castles, stately homes, abbeys, ancient monuments, nature reserves, waterfalls and notable viewpoints. The 'centres' that are listed range from cities of more than 500,000 population down to villages of less than 2,000, but at all there is more than one chance of finding an inn or hotel with room.

1

NATIONAL PARKS

⟶ ◦ ◦ ⟶

The first national park is now one hundred years old. In 1872 the United States Congress passed an Act setting apart a region in the States of Montana and Wyoming as 'a public park or pleasuring ground for the benefit and enjoyment of the people'. This was Yellowstone Park, nearly as large as all seven English national parks put together. The Act went on to prohibit settlement in this park and laid down that it should be looked after by the Secretary of the Interior.

This piece of original legislation arose through the efforts of two Americans who, struck by the natural beauty of the area, were determined that it should not suffer from the exploitation which they knew had already disfigured parts of the continent. The idea spread quickly into the neighbouring new country of Canada, where the first similar park was declared at Banff in 1885. Like Yellowstone it had an area of hot springs, and in this they both resembled the much earlier national reservation of Hot Springs, Arkansas, where, in 1832, an area of 1,000 acres was dedicated by Congress 'to recreation and the restoration of the Health of the American people'.

Perhaps one thousand rather than one hundred years ago this country could have adopted the same pattern for national parks. But by the nineteenth century the land of England and Wales had undergone clearance, settlement, cultivation, enclosure and the Industrial Revolution. In few areas would it have been possible to set aside even 1,000 acres of natural wilderness for the people. Nevertheless, in 1889 a leader in the *Manchester Guardian* was calling for the nationalisation of the Lake District and, failing that, suggesting with some imagination the shape our national parks might take: 'If the cost of nationalising be beyond the pockets of the wealthy English, surely we could demand a ministerial conservancy, to interfere with the property owners only when their acts were plainly antagonistic to the higher interests of the people.'

Over the next fifty years the movement for national parks became closely linked with the pressures for more public access to mountains. Bills introduced in 1908, 1924, 1926 and 1927 attempted to clear this first summit but were beaten back by adverse conditions in Parliament; withdrawn, lost in committee or balked by 'the congested state of business', none made much progress. But public feeling was growing, and in 1932 a mass trespass organised on Kinder Scout achieved more publicity than the host of parliamentary measures that had gone before. Fighting with keepers took place, arrests were made and some prison sentences passed. The Access to Mountains Act eventually reached the statute book in 1939 but had been so amended in committee as to emerge with severe shortcomings.

Meanwhile a number of government reports came and went, all recommending some form of national park, and Planning Acts in 1925 and 1932 provided the cause of rural preservation with some crumbs of comfort. So when, in 1939, another sort of war broke out, there was, even during the darkest days, some prospect that peace would bring progress. A Committee under Lord Justice Scott stated roundly that 'the establishment of national parks in Britain is long overdue'. That was in 1942, and in 1943 a new Ministry of Town and Country Planning was formed, taking over this subject from the Ministry of Health.

It was the new Minister of Town and Country Planning who announced that he had asked John Dower, an architect, to make a study of the problems involved in establishing national parks in England and Wales. The report that resulted has a secure place in national park history, for its farsighted proposals formed the basis of nearly everything that has followed. In particular John Dower's definition of our national parks is still the best:

> an extensive area of beautiful and relatively wild country in which, for the nation's benefit and by appropriate national decision and action, (a) the characteristic landscape beauty is strictly preserved, (b) access and facilities for public openair enjoyment are amply provided, (c) wild life and buildings and places of architectural and historic interest are suitably protected, while (d) established farming use is effectively maintained.

Ten areas were suggested for national parks, together with a reserve list of a dozen and a list of other amenity areas where action was needed.

In 1945, the year of the Dower Report, a new Committee was set up under Sir Arthur Hobhouse to consider the detailed application of the recommendations. This Committee, which reported in 1947, set out a scheme for the selection, planning and management of national parks and the protection of other areas of outstanding landscape value as conservation areas. A list of parks, differing slightly from that of John Dower, was set out in three instalments, four parks to be designated in each of three successive years. All the present parks were included, together with the South Downs and the Norfolk Broads. The list of conservation areas has formed the basis of the designation programme for areas of outstanding natural beauty. Neither the Dower nor the Hobhouse Report considered it essential that all, or even a great part, of the land in a park should be taken into public ownership, though acquisition of land might be necessary in some places for reclamation or improvement, or for nature reserves, or to provide sites for hostels or other holiday accommodation.

The Hobhouse Report coincided with the introduction of new planning legislation in the Town and Country Planning Act 1947, and both had an influence on the eventual shape of the National Parks and Access to the Countryside Act of 1949. A National Parks Commission was set up, as recommended in the Hobhouse Report, but without the powers that had been proposed in that report, while responsibility for the planning of park areas was to be entrusted to the county councils who had just taken on this function from district councils. It was a compromise solution and was criticized as such at the time, but over a period of twenty years it has seen the establishment and growth of a system of national parks and other designated areas that has considerable merits.*

In 1968 new legislation under the Countryside Act helped to put the national parks in a context of countrywide conservation and provision for people's leisure and recreation. There was recognition that growth in the amount of people's leisure and their mobility required new provisions. The Countryside Commission replaced the old National Parks Commission and took on a number of new jobs, including the setting up, in conjunction with local authorities and others, of a network of country parks.

One characteristic shared by all the national parks is a high proportion of open country. The definition of open country contained in the 1949 Act is 'mountain, moor, heath, down, cliff or foreshore' and it excludes all agricultural land other than rough grazing. So the national parks tend to be predominantly upland areas and occur in the north and west of England, and in Wales, rather than in the more intensively cultivated south and east. The Cotswolds and the South Downs, for instance, have not become national parks for this reason, though both of these beautiful areas have been accorded another form of protective designation. On the other hand an area of mid Wales picked out in the earliest reports has seen comparatively little change until recently and has now been proposed as an eleventh national park, the Cambrian Mountains National Park, so as to protect the future of its fine uplands.

When an area is selected as a national park there is, as we have noted, no change in the ownership of land. Nor is there any special right of access for walkers, climbers or riders, or for picnicking. In our national parks, which are quite unlike the vast natural reserves established by less intensively

* Under the Local Government Act 1972 arrangements for the administration of national parks are being changed. In future the planning of each park will be the responsibility of a single executive committee or board, each will have its own national park officer, and a greater part of the expenditure will be contributed by central government.

developed countries, people live and work and continue to own land. Some land is owned by the Forestry Commission, who may have Forest Parks within (Snowdonia) or adjoining (Border) national parks; some land is owned and managed as national nature reserves; quite large areas, particularly in the Lake District, are protected by the National Trust; in some places land has been acquired by the park authority. But the bulk remains in private ownership, and is as private in a national park as anywhere else.

The park authorities have the duty of protecting the landscape beauty of the parks for our enjoyment. Working through the normal processes of planning control they set high standards, attending particularly to design and materials, and the siting and screening of any development; they may refuse permission if it seems unsuitable for its national park setting. Their other main task is to make sure that people are able to enjoy what is being protected in this way for them. The provision of parking places, picnic, camping and caravan sites, negotiation of public access to open country, the laying out of footpaths and nature trails—these are some of the actions which the park authorities under-take with grant aid from the government. They also run warden and informa-tion services. A visit to any of the parks described in this book could well begin with a call at the most convenient park information centre.

Parc Cenedlaethol Bannau Brycheinog
The Brecon Beacons

In 1957 the last of the ten national parks of England and Wales was designated. The Brecon Beacons National Park covers 519 square miles, most of
it in Breconshire, but with its western and eastern ends in Carmarthenshire
and Monmouthshire. In shape rather like a generously elongated shoulder of
Welsh mutton, it extends from Hay-on-Wye and Abergavenny on the Usk
westwards to Llandovery and Llandeilo in the Vale of Tywi. To the south
the Heads of the Valleys Road separates it dramatically from the smoky
trenches of industrial South Wales, while to the north its boundary is formed
by the valley of the Usk and by the scarp of the Black Mountains.

This is indeed an area of great scarps and ridged mountain and moorland,
roughly split into four massive blocks ranged side by side from west to east.
Most westerly is the Black Mountain (singular) rising to 2460 feet and 2632
feet in the Carmarthen Fan and the Brecknock Fan. Next to it comes Fforest
Fawr, formerly the Great Forest of Brecknock and a royal hunting-ground,
with the line of summits running through its centre from the Brecknock
Fan to Fan Fawr (2409 feet). On the other side of the Brecon-Merthyr road the
moorland rises again, this time to the Beacons proper and the crested summits
of Pen y Fan (2906 feet) and Corn Du (2863 feet). The last block lies across
the Usk—the Black Mountains (plural) of the Breconshire-Monmouthshire
borders with their steep northern face looking out over the broad valley of the
Wye. A few smaller areas to the south and east complete the geography of the
park: the moorlands of Llangynidr and Llangattock, the massive Blorenge
(1833 feet) overlooking Abergavenny, the Skirrid (1596 feet), and an extension down the line of the Monmouthshire and Brecon Canal almost to
Pontypool.

The basic geological structure of the park area is relatively simple since it
forms the northern flank of the South Wales coalfield. The rocks dip from
north to south towards the basin of the coalfield, and their outcrops thus
strike east-west, as indicated by the impressive escarpments mentioned above.
The Old Red Sandstone, a series of rocks of vast thickness made up of flag-
stones, marls, sandstones, grits and conglomerates, is responsible for most of
the park's landscape and for nearly all the higher land. In the north-west
corner the older Silurian and Ordovician rocks appear from beneath it over
a small area between Llandovery and Llandeilo, and along the southern edge
of the park the Old Red Sandstone dips in turn beneath younger rocks—

The Honddu Valley in the Black Mountains. In the centre of the picture are the ruins of Llanthony Priory.

Carboniferous limestone, Millstone Grit and the base of the Coal Measures. The limestone area is particularly interesting; because of its position at the foot of a long dip-slope draining a heavy rainfall from acid moorlands it has become riddled with sink-holes, caves and underground channels, including the longest known cave system in Britain.

The characteristic flat tops of the highest mountains in the park are the result of a bed of hard conglomerate which has protected the more vulnerable mixture of hard and soft bands below. Their steep faces with deep north-facing hollows or *cwms* are an indication of ice action. It is likely that during the Ice Age the ice cap covered most of the area, for the debris left by glaciers is found high up among the hills. The largest glacier occupied the present Usk Valley, where it scooped out the hollow that now forms Llangorse Lake, damming it with clay and gravel. In the warmer times following the retreat of the ice, trees and other vegetation spread upwards to all but the highest slopes, according to those experts who have studied the evidence offered by the succession of peat deposits on the uplands. Remains of bear, wild ox and red

26

The Sugar Loaf seen from the approach to Hatteral Ridge.

deer have been found in cave deposits in the park, but it probably remained
for long an area hunted rather than settled by man.

What follows is a common history of those upland areas that form our
national parks: a gradual clearance of woodland either for cultivation or to
provide timber and fuel for industry. Grazing by cattle and later much more
by sheep has prevented any reversion to scrub and woodland, and has added
to the bare higher slopes a much larger area of rough pasture and grazing,
often invaded by bracken. In this park a large proportion of the upland has
been common grazing land since mediaeval times. Farmers on the more fertile
valleysides send their sheep and cattle on to the commons to supplement their
own enclosed pastures, and some also maintain the herds of 'wild' ponies
often seen there. These commons are a feature of the park that makes it an
ideal place for the walker and pony-trekker; besides giving good access to
extensive areas of the higher land it has preserved them from too much fencing
or forestry.

Walkers and riders will as usual get the most out of the park's landscape

27

The summit of the Sugar Loaf, with the Skirrid in the background.

by way of the high-level routes along the Beacons, the 'darens' or sandstone ridges of the Black Mountains, and on the Black Mountain of Carmarthen-shire. On these one can travel for miles always above the 2000-foot contour, with fine views northwards across the broad valleys of Usk and Wye to the mountains of Mid Wales or southward across the hidden settlements of the coalfields to the Bristol Channel. But there are also some fine roads crossing the park through the main clefts: besides the main through routes such as Brynamman to Llangadog, Ystradgynlais to Sennybridge, Merthyr to Brecon, and Crickhowell to Talgarth, there are some more spectacular high crossings by the minor roads like that between Pontneddvechan to Heol Senni via Ystradfellte, the Gospel Pass that crosses the Black Mountains scarp from the Honddu Valley to Hay-on-Wye, or from Dowlais to Talybont by way of two of the park's larger reservoirs, Taf Fechan and Talybont.

In this largely unspoiled landscape which gains in attraction through proximity to industrial South Wales, reservoirs are to be expected, since that

28

The River Usk, looking west from Llangynidr Bridge.

area has largely polluted its own supplies. The main ones send water to Newport, Cardiff and Swansea, and perhaps the park authorities should count it good fortune that the Beacons are not asked to supply water for even farther afield. In Brecon Museum details can be seen of an ambitious late nineteenth-century scheme which would have flooded a large part of the park in the Usk Valley to supply London with Welsh water via two great aqueducts branching to either side of the Thames basin!

Though there are many fine routes over the area of the park, they often traverse upland regions where settlements are few. Most people out on a day

Cwmyoy Village in the Black Mountains. Landslips have cleft the hillside and oddly tilted
St. Martin's Church (centre).

Porth yr Ogof—the entrance to the cave, near Ystradfellte.

or half-day visit like to have a fixed destination to aim for, and this must have contributed to the success of the Brecon Beacons Mountain Centre. The Centre stands over 1000 feet up at the edge of Mynydd Illtud Common looking across Glyn Tarell to the Beacons, has a free car park, a comfortable lounge and terrace with panoramic views, an information point, refreshment room, and facilities for field studies and outdoor pursuits. Not surprisingly it has become very popular, with something like 200,000 visitors a year, including a substantial use outside the holiday season, for it is open daily throughout the year, except for Christmas Day.

Like the park's information centres at Abergavenny, Brecon and Llandovery, the Mountain Centre helps to introduce to visitors the richness and variety of the national park through displays, maps and leaflets. The park has much to attract those with an interest in history and antiquities, for instance. There are hill fortifications in commanding overlook positions at Crucywel (Table Mountain) above the town of the same name, Crickhowell, and above the road from there to Talgarth at Castell Dinas, nearly 1500 feet up, while close to Brecon there is a third, Pen-y-Crug, which also provides a fine viewpoint for those who climb its ramparts and ditches. Also near Brecon is Y Gaer, an excavated Roman fort. Among Norman strongholds marking the advance of their power along the Usk Valley, Tretower Castle is an interesting example, with a round tower keep inside the remains of the older

'An area of great scarps and ridged mountain and moorland': the carved summit ridge of the Beacons seen from the east.

The Welsh fortress of Carreg Cennen in the Carmarthenshire section of the park.

Norman work. Nearby stands Tretower Court, the well preserved mediaeval manor house which replaced the more cramped quarters of the castle. A quite different kind of fortress is to be seen at the western end of the park where Carreg Cennen, for long a Welsh stronghold, clings to a 300-foot limestone cliff. Of ecclesiastical buildings the massive cathedral church of St John at Brecon, the ruins of Llanthony Priory in the Honddu Valley, and the tiny church of Partrishow—so isolated among the narrow lanes at the foot of the

Grwyne Fawr valley that it has preserved some surprising treasures, including an exquisitely carved rood screen—are three that most people would not wish to miss.

There are three national nature reserves in the park. Craig Cerrig-Gleisiad, of nearly 700 acres, has moorland and two sandstone crags, and contains arctic-alpine plants, the most southerly in Britain. By contrast Cwm Clydach, six miles south-west of Abergavenny, has two mature beech woods in its fifty acres. Craig y Ciliau, two miles south-west of Crickhowell, is a Carboniferous Limestone outcrop with some interesting tree species, as well as the entrance to the Agen Allwedd cave system, the most extensive in the country. Permits are needed to visit this and the other reserves, but for those wishing to see something of the underground world of the park there are show caves at Dan yr Ogof, which lies not far from Craig y Nos.

Finally, one unique feature of the park is the Monmouthshire and Brecon Canal, which runs for thirty-two miles, mostly contouring the mountainside above the Usk Valley from Brecon to Pontypool, just outside the park. Now used exclusively for pleasure cruising and greatly improved through a programme of works organised by British Waterways Board with the park authority and the Countryside Commission, it also provides a delightful towpath walk.

The Brecon Beacons National Park is run by three separate committees—one for each of the counties of Breconshire, Carmarthenshire and Monmouthshire—with a joint advisory committee for the whole park. The park symbol is, appropriately, a lighted beacon, the base incorporating a shield with a Welsh dragon.

CENTRES   Abergavenny, Brecon, Crickhowell, Llandovery, Aberdare

PLACES OF INTEREST   Agen Allwedd, Brecon (cathedral church), Brecon Mountain Centre, Bronllys Castle, Capel-y-ffin (monastery and chapel), Carreg Cennen Castle, Castell Dinas, Crickhowell (bridge and castle), Crug Hywel (hill-fort), Cwmyoy Church, Dan yr Ogof, Y Gaer (Roman fort), Hay Castle, Llaneleu Church, Llangorse Lake, Llanthony Priory, Ogof Ffynnon Ddu, Partrishow Church, Pen-y-Crug (hill-fort), Porth yr Ogof, Skirrid, Sugar Loaf, Tretower (Castle and Court)

Dartmoor

The last great wilderness of southern Britain, Dartmoor is an extraordinary museum in many ways. This high moorland plateau has preserved its landscape almost unchanged since prehistoric times, a setting for the hundreds of ancient monuments and other traces of man's three thousand years or more of occupation of the moor. In September 1950 members of the National Parks Commission, then less than one year old, visited Dartmoor to study the area and review boundaries for a national park that would add some legislative protection to the existing physical and geographical defences of the moor. After consultations with the local authorities, and a second visit, they designated the park the following August, making it the fourth park to be established.

A rough quadrilateral in shape, the park covers 365 square miles and includes the framework of more pastoral land surrounding the moor itself. East to west it stretches from Bovey Tracey to Tavistock, and north to south from Okehampton to Ivybridge. Two main roads—Ashburton to Tavistock and Yelverton to Moretonhampstead—cross in the centre of the park at Two Bridges, but vast areas of Dartmoor are roadless, not to say trackless.

The harsh moorland landscape, over 200 square miles in extent, coincides almost exactly with the outcrop of Dartmoor granite. This core of hard granite was pushed up under the surface rocks during a period of mountain-building 240 million years ago, and the rocks covering it were then worn away. Around the core lie rocks altered and hardened by the original heat of the granite mass; these can be seen in some of the spectacular 'cleaves' or gorges by which the streams and rivers of Dartmoor leave the granite moorland. The granite itself is easily seen in the 'tors', resistant masses capping many of the higher areas of moorland and often worn into fantastic shapes as at Haytor and Bowerman's Nose, as well as in the 'clitters', patches of shattered granite blocks, the result of the breaking down of exposed rock by the action of snow and ice.

Dartmoor is, of course, notorious for its mists. Prevailing winds blowing over 4000 miles of the Atlantic lift moist air over the western lip of the moor, bringing low cloud and a heavy rainfall as well. In these conditions rivers and streams can rise rapidly to become plunging torrents of peaty brown water, but the general low relief of the moor and the presence of two large areas of blanket bog also enable it to act as a sponge. Nearly all the rivers of Devon have their source on Dartmoor. On the eastern fringes of the park, away

The West Dart River and Huccaby Bridge.

from the immediate lee of the high land, the rainfall is appreciably lower. The highest land is in the west and north where High Willhays and nearby Yes Tor are over 2000 feet, but nearly the whole of the moor lies at between 1000 and 1500 feet above sea level. For visitors from the South Devon coastal resorts this is worth remembering, for average Dartmoor temperatures are as much as 5 degrees F. lower than at Torquay. But it is a place of extremes in climate and can as easily be hot and shadeless as cold and wet.

It was probably the treelessness of Dartmoor that attracted settlers in the Bronze Age, when the moorland was drier and there was less peat bog. Secure above the forest land which surrounded the moor and penetrated up the valleys, they lived, worked and worshipped. Today, evidence of all three activities remains to be seen all over the moor, undisturbed by any later cultivation. There are hut circles, pounds—most notably Grimspound where a 6-foot wall encloses twenty-four small huts—stone circles such as the Grey Wethers north of Postbridge and that at Scorhill near Gidleigh, and stone rows or avenues of which there is a fine example two miles north-east of Cornwood in an area of the park simply packed with ancient monuments. Most numerous of all are the various remains of burials and tombs, from megaliths of the New Stone Age, like Spinster's Rock near Drewsteignton, to Bronze Age cairns and tumuli. Hill forts of later, Iron Age, times can also be seen in the Drewsteignton area: Prestonbury Castle has a fine position overlooking Fingle Bridge. Clapper bridges, those massive slabs of granite laid end to end across piers of the same material, are, despite their primeval appearance, generally of much later date than the antiquities mentioned above. Many of them were erected by the tin miners of mediaeval times.

Reminders of the tin industry on Dartmoor, which started as early as the twelfth century, are to be found in many parts of the moor. Like the ancient monuments they not only provide features of interest for those exploring the moor on foot, but are also the source of many of its ancient tracks. There are 'blowing houses' where the tinners smelted ore in small furnaces before taking the tin to the Stannary Towns for assay and the payment of Crown duty. There were four Stannary Towns—Tavistock, Plympton, Ashburton and Chagford—and the strict stannary laws were enacted by a tinners' parliament which met from time to time on the summit of Crockern Tor, not far from Two Bridges and almost at the centre of the moor. The great stone keep of Lydford Castle, built in 1195, was notorious as the prison into which were thrown any suspected of offending against these or the forest laws of Dartmoor, often without the benefit of a trial.

Opposite, top: Old clapper bridge at Postbridge.
   below: Combestone Tor and the view towards Dartmeet.

Brentor, and the twelfth-century church of St Michael perched on its volcanic crag.

Dartmoor Prison, at Princetown, has altogether different origins. A prison was first built there not because the moor offered a high-security site but as a work camp during the Napoleonic Wars for prisoners of war from the hulks anchored in Plymouth Sound. Here they could be employed in taming the wild moor and in quarrying granite. After the wars the prison closed, to be reopened in 1850 as a convict settlement. The name Princetown commemorates the gift of land for the first prison by the Prince of Wales, then as now landlord of the Duchy of Cornwall, which has owned most of Dartmoor ever since the thirteenth century. On the other side of the moor, not far from Haytor, lies another area of granite quarrying and the remains of an early horse-operated railway with tracks made from granite setts, now half-hidden in the heather. In the 1820s granite was taken from here to the coast and shipped to London, where it was later used for the old London Bridge, now spanning the River Colorado in America.

38

The hardy Blackface sheep face rough weather on the Moor.

Haytor, one of the most accessible of Dartmoor's granite tors.

From Haytor, which can more easily be approached by car than most Dartmoor tors, there are fine views of the coast and the Teign estuary and also of the eastern fringes of the national park. Here lie some of the best-known villages, such as Buckland and Widecombe in the Moor, North Bovey and Manaton, as well as well-visited spots like Buckfast Abbey, Becka Falls, and Dartmeet, where the East and West Dart Rivers meet to flow through a thickly wooded gorge. A comparable viewpoint on the western side of the park is Brentor, a volcanic crag crowned by the tiny twelfth-century church of St Michael. Nearby is the impressive ravine of Lydford Gorge, through which a series of paths, on National Trust land, leads to the rapids and waterfalls of the Lyd and its tributaries.

Despite the apparently sparse nature of the grazings, Dartmoor carries stocks of animals in quite large number. The native breed of sheep, the Whitefaced Dartmoor, is now less common than the Scottish Blackface, which can be seen on the moor most of the year round. Cattle are less often turned on to the moor, even in summer, but again the hardy Scottish breeds such as Galloways, and occasionally Highland Cattle, are sometimes to be

The village of Widecombe in the Moor.

An old farmhouse and, in the background, Holne Woods on the fringe of the Moor.

seen. Most noticeable of all, however, are the Dartmoor ponies. These are not true wild horses, their ancestors probably being stock turned loose over a thousand years ago; they are very variable in colour and are relatively easily broken in to become popular mounts for children. The ponies belong to farmers and others with grazing rights on the moor, and are annually rounded up in 'Pony Drifts' for branding.

For the naturalist the main interest of the national park is in the relict vegetation. There are three national nature reserves and two forest nature reserves, of which the best known is Wistman's Wood, two miles up the West Dart from Two Bridges. Here, protected by enormous granite boulders,

42

Wistman's Wood, a forest nature reserve of relict oak growing amongst granite boulders.

a small oak wood has survived, its trees grotesquely twisted and moss-covered.

The best way to see Dartmoor is undoubtedly to walk or ride over it. Roads are comparatively few and narrow; they easily fill with cars and coaches which can also quickly make the landscape appear crowded. The national park authority, faced with some four million visitors a year, and summer Sundays when 195,000 cars can enter the park, have constructed a plan to control traffic to certain areas, reserving others for quieter enjoyment. Of the other problems faced by the park authority, the three most serious are water, china clay and the military presence in the north-west of the park. There has been considerable resistance to the siting of further reservoirs in the park since the battle to preserve the Meldon Valley against flooding was lost. A scheme for a large reservoir at Swincombe in the heart of the southern moorland was rejected by a select committee of Parliament in 1970. The massive china clay excavations lie just outside the park boundary in the south-west at Lee Moor, where it is easy to see what damage could be done to the park's landscape by any extension of digging or tipping into an attractive and accessible area of the moor. The army has been on Dartmoor since long before it became a national park; they use a large part of the high ground from the edge of Okehampton to Great Mis Tor for training exercises and artillery practice, also maintaining a rifle range at Rippon Tor in the east. While the Services using these areas try to make them accessible to the public whenever possible, the fact remains that their continued presence there is incompatible with the status of the land as a national park. Notices giving dates and times of firing are displayed in Post Offices all over the park but anyone on an unplanned visit to the areas mentioned above is advised to keep well clear when the red flags are flying.

The park authority is the Dartmoor National Park Committee, a separate committee of Devon County Council, composed of ten county councillors, two members from district councils, and six members nominated by the Secretary of State for the Environment. They use the planning and other services of the county council and maintain an information service at Two Bridges during the summer months. The park symbol is a Dartmoor pony on a hexagonal background.

CENTRES   Ashburton, Bovey Tracey, Buckfastleigh, Exeter, Moretonhampstead, Newton Abbot, Okehampton, Plymouth, Tavistock

PLACES OF INTEREST   Brentor, Buckfast Abbey, Buckland in the Moor, Chagford, Cranmere Pool, Dartmeet, Drewsteignton, Fingle Bridge, Bidleigh Castle, Grimspound, Haytor, Lydford Castle, Lydford Gorge, Manaton, North Bovey, Postbridge, Okehampton Castle, Throwleigh, Two Bridges, Widecombe in the Moor, Wistman's Wood, Yes Tor

Exmoor

The smallest of England's seven national parks, Exmoor is nevertheless packed with interest and variety, 'infinite riches in a little room'. From Brendon Common, an open area near the centre of the park, is unfolded a panorama of the high tableland of Exmoor, miles of grass and heather moorland intersected by deep combes. Scarcely five miles away at Countisbury Common, is as fine a view of Exmoor's coastline, with the great beak of Foreland, the moor plunging abruptly towards the sea in a line of hogsback cliffs, and a steep road descending to Lynmouth.

The 265 square miles of the park were designated in 1954. From the coastline between Minehead's North Hill and Combe Martin across the Devon border, the park extends inland as much as fourteen miles, including the South Exmoor centre of Dulverton. Besides the main block of Exmoor, a plateau generally between 1000 feet and 1500 feet above sea level except for Dunkery Beacon (1705 feet), the outlying Brendon Hills and Selworthy Beacon are also in the park.

Selworthy Beacon is separated from the main part of Exmoor by a narrow basin stretching inland from Porlock Bay, an area of green fields and a red soil that indicates the presence of the New Red Sandstone underneath. This kind of landscape is not repeated elsewhere in the park where the underlying rock is almost entirely made up of a series of grits, slates, shales, sandstone and limestone of equivalent age to the Old Red Sandstone which makes up the Brecon Beacons national park. These rocks are folded and tilted steeply away from the sea—it is this that produces the hogsback cliffs—so that their outcrops run in broad bands along the length of the park and at a slight angle to the coast, giving there an east-west succession from older to newer rocks. The rivers that drain northwards into the Bristol Channel have short steep courses. The West Lyn, for instance, drops as much as 400 feet in its last mile, a factor which, with the phenomenally high rainfall, contributed to the suddenness of Lynmouth's disastrous flooding in 1952. Those draining southwards flow more gently, through wooded combes into the Barle and Exe, which meet just outside the park at Exebridge. Like most high land close to the Atlantic coasts, the heights of Exmoor attract a heavy rainfall, up to sixty inches a year, not much lower than Dartmoor's.

'A filthy, barren ground' wrote William Camden of Exmoor in the seventeenth century, and is echoed by a later commentator: 'a damp barren forest partly in Devon but chiefly in Somerset'. What both are referring to is

The rocky 'cleave' of Waters Meet on the East Lyn River.

The harbour at Lynmouth.

central Exmoor, the old Royal Forest that lies around Simonsbath, its capital. Until the nineteenth century the Forest remained a wilderness area, although grazed in summer according to ancient rights. There were just a few enclosures around Simonsbath, the enterprise of James Boevey, builder of the hunting lodge there at the time of the Commonwealth when royal lands were being sold off. It was a Midlands ironmaster, John Knight, and his family, who were in a large way responsible for the landscape of this part of Exmoor as we see it today—a pattern in which farms and fields break up the areas of moorland. The remains can still be seen of the great wall which

Woody Bay and Duty Point on the steeply plunging coast of Exmoor.

Knight built round his estate. He experimented with different kinds of husbandry and established the system of stock farming that has survived all changes in agricultural fortunes to the present day. True to their past, the Knights also looked for iron, which occurs sporadically throughout Exmoor along an east-west line from the Brendon Hills, but without much success.

The improvements effected by the Knights and others did not, however, greatly disturb the higher areas of moorland or remove from the scene the traces of earlier inhabitants that are to be found on these as on other uplands. An ancient trackway along the ridge that marks the county boundary between Devon and Somerset makes what is probably the finest high-level walk in the park. Along it lie barrows of Bronze Age date, and not far away is a conspicuous monument of the same age, the 9-foot Long Stone, near Challacombe. Another famous Exmoor stone is the Caratacus Stone, an inscribed pillar believed to date from the Dark Ages, on Winsford Hill. Perhaps the most impressive of a number of British forts within the park is Shoulsbarrow, again near Challacombe, with a fine double rampart wall enclosing nearly ten acres in all. An early date is sometimes ascribed to Tarr Steps, the primitive stone bridge over the Barle near the village of

48

Combe Martin Bay and Hangman Hill at the western end of the park.

Hawkridge, but like the clapper bridges of Dartmoor, which it resembles, it is more likely to be mediaeval in origin. On the coast are remains of two Roman signal stations—one on the cliffs at Martinhoe and the other near County Gate. Dunkery too was probably part of a system of warning beacons from the earliest times, and its light must have been visible right across the county of Devon to the Channel.

The present-day settlements of Exmoor are villages of no great size, serving a community mostly engaged in farming, though the one-time ports on the few accessible parts of the coast have grown with the holiday trade, and inland holidays, particularly pony-trekking, are now becoming more popular. Dunster, in the east, has the legacy of a once thriving woollen industry in its Yarn Market and fine main street, overlooked by the Castle which has been in the Luttrell family for the last 600 years. Winsford (Ernest Bevin's village) and Selworthy, much of which is owned by the National Trust, are noted for their thatch and cob architecture. Lynton and Lynmouth, much of the latter rebuilt after the flood disaster, are justly popular holiday centres; Porlock and Porlock Weir, on the edge of the richest farmland in the park, were, like Lynmouth, places for trade across the Bristol Channel to South Wales.

49

Dunkery Beacon and the moorland plateau.

If farming is the main occupation of those who live and work in the park, hunting also ranks high in importance. On Exmoor, hunting means not only the fox but the red deer. These magnificent beasts, the largest British land mammals, whose antlers provide the national park with its sign, are indeed one of the park's chief glories. The Exmoor herds, descendants of the native red deer of prehistoric times, inhabit the scrub woodlands of the combes but

50

Tarr Steps, the ancient bridge across the River Barle.

also roam over the moor and over farmland, where they can do much damage to crops. Many farmers are prepared to put up with losses to root crops in return for the sport afforded by the hunt, and but for the protection the deer get in this way they might well have become extinct with the disappearance of the Royal Forest. Although the red deer population is normally over 500, the animals are not always easy to spot. On the moor the best time to see them is in spring, when they are attracted into the open country by the new growth of grass.

Almost as well known as the red deer are the Exmoor ponies. Like the deer, these may well be descendants of genuine wild stock, for the pure Exmoor has the powerful head, dun colouring and short mane in common with the East European wild horses. Though owned by the local farms, the ponies run wild on the moor and mostly find their own food. Rounded up and broken in, they make good mounts for children and provide the local riding and pony trekking stables with beasts that really know the terrain. Dulverton and Exford are good centres for riding and for the hunt.

It would be hard to say how many, out of the thousands who visit 'the

Looking from Grabbist Hill towards the eastern edge of the park, with Dunster and its castle in the foreground.

Doone Country', had previously read R. D. Blackmore's tale of *Lorna Doone*, or whether many return from their visit to read it. But certainly the Doone legends feature among Exmoor's tourist attractions, and, since everyone likes a good romance, *Lorna Doone* retains its popularity. Blackmore called his book a 'Romance of Exmoor' because, he wrote, 'the incidents, characters, time and scenery are alike romantic'. But the lively detail of his story and its descriptions of Exmoor have led many to try to trace exact locations for the places mentioned in it; and since Blackmore used a fair amount of artistic licence, there are many arguments about this. The Hoccombe valley opening off Badgworthy Water is generally taken as the home of the villainous Doones; it is a lengthy but interesting walk from Malmsmead. The little church at Oare, scene of the wedding of Lorna with John Ridd, when the bride was shot at the altar steps by Carver Doone, is much more accessible, and it is reckoned that upwards of 50,000 people visit it every year.

The landscape of Exmoor National Park gains much of its appeal from the way in which the rough moorland is interspersed with wooded combes

'Grass and heather moorland intersected by deep combes': the Brendon Valley from Countisbury Hill.

and fringed with patchwork farm land around the scattered farmsteads. This pattern of land use and the proportion of open land has been threatened by further reclamation of the heather moor by ploughing and fencing and for afforestation. The park planning authorities therefore carried out a survey a few years ago, identifying just over a quarter of the park's acreage as being of critical amenity value, of which in turn nearly one quarter was protected by National Trust or local authority ownership. Provision was made under the Countryside Act for an 'early warning system' where ploughing and enclosure of open land were being considered, and for compensation to be paid in cases where public access could be agreed. A proposal to plant the Chains, a grim area in the centre of the moorland, with trees was never pursued, and indeed the area might well have proved intractable. On the whole, a policy of woodland based on the existing areas which follow the lower slopes of the combes and do not encroach on the open moor is the only one acceptable to the character of the park. The park authorities purchased a critical area of coppiced oak, beech, ash and birch woodland above Porlock to manage it for amenity purposes; here, in Hawkcombe Woods, waymarked walks and rides have been set out, extending from the village below to the open moors above.

Committees of Devon and Somerset County Councils are the planning authorities for the park, and there is a joint advisory committee of twelve (five from Somerset, three from Devon, and four nominated by the Secretary of State for the Environment and appointed by the county councils jointly). Park information centres are at Minehead and Combe Martin, thus covering both ends of the park, and also at the Lyn and Exmoor Museum, Lynton.

CENTRES   Combe Martin, Dulverton, Exford, Ilfracombe, Lynton/Lynmouth, Minehead, Porlock

PLACES OF INTEREST   Badgworthy Water, Brendon, Chapman Barrows, Countisbury, Culbone Church, Dunkery Beacon, Dunster (and Castle), Five Barrows, Holwell Castle, Landacre Bridge, Nettlecombe Court, Oare Church, Parracombe, Porlock Weir, Selworthy, Shoulsbarrow Castle, Simonsbath, Stoke Pero Church, Tarr Steps, Valley of the Rocks, Waters Meet, Winsford, Withypool, Woody Bay

The Lake District

＜二＞

'A sort of National Property in which every man has a right and interest who has an eye to perceive and a heart to enjoy.' Wordsworth's phrase, from his guide to the Lakes, was given new meaning when, in 1951, the Lake District became the second of the country's national parks. It is still the largest: 866 square miles, stretching from Cartmel in the south to Caldbeck in the north, from Ravenglass on the coast to Shap in the east. The park is a rough square in shape, its south-west to north-east diagonal running from Silecroft to Pooley Bridge, both just inside the boundary, and south-east to north-west from Kendal to Cockermouth, both just outside.

From any one of a dozen fine viewpoints in the central fells it is easy to appreciate the compactness of the Lake District; on a reasonably clear day one can see beyond the boundaries of the park. At the same time the general pattern of the mountainous area becomes apparent—the high ground broken into ridges by the deep valleys, and the long fingers of the lakes running out towards the foothills. For geologically the Lake District is a gentle dome. The conventionally coloured geological map also helps to make the pattern clearer. A ragged framework of Cambridge blue surrounds the national park area. This is the Carboniferous Limestone, showing itself in the long scars of Whitbarrow, the hills of Furness and the country around Kendal. Outside it lies the rose-pink of the Permian and Triassic sandstones, seen at St Bees Head and Penrith Beacon. Three broad belts coloured light grey, pink and blue-grey fill the centre: in the north the Skiddaw Slates, in the south the Silurian rocks, and in the middle the resistant rocks of the Borrowdale Volcanic Series.

The effect of the rocks on the mountain forms is again easy to distinguish. The Skiddaw Slate region has smooth-sided and rounded outlines with long scree-slopes contrasting with the rough, craggy scenery of the Central and Eastern fells, while in the southern part of the park an altogether gentler landscape results from the underlying slates and limestones. The obviously radial drainage pattern of the Lake District is a legacy of the original domed structure, but another important influence on the scenery has been the Ice Age. The most striking evidence of the ancient glaciers is in the broad, steep-sided valleys dwarfing their present streams, tributary valleys left 'hanging', often with fine waterfalls now plunging into the main valley, and in the scooped-out hollows, some now filled with dark tarns.

55

Honister Crag and the view towards the Buttermere Valley.

The lakes themselves are a stage in the decline of the Ice Age, a quite transitory feature when set against even the scale of archaeological, let alone geological, time. The twelve main lakes occupy valleys where glaciers over-deepened the floors and blocked drainage with their debris. But the streams and rivers work hard to get rid of the lakes, cutting away at the lake-foot obstructions (wherever these are not helped by the dams of water engineers) and filling the lake-heads with rocks, pebbles and silt. At Buttermere and Derwentwater small deltas can be seen as examples of this filling in, while in Kentmere valley, once the possessor of two lakes, the process has been com-pleted, and the lower of the two lake-bed sites now provides a source of valuable diatomite, the remains of tiny organisms that once inhabited it.

The Lake District is sometimes taken as an example of an unspoilt, pri-meval wilderness area, where nature alone has held sway. But since the end of

Waterfall at Stanley Ghyll above Eskdale; public access to the fall has been bought by the park authority.

Scafell Pike, the highest mountain in England, seen from the summit of Bow Fell.

the Ice Age, the most far-reaching changes to the landscape have been the work of man. Much of the forest that once covered all but the highest ground was cleared, first by settlers, then for charcoal and fuel for furnaces of the mineral industry. Grazing animals, particularly sheep, kept down the growth and produced the bare, grassy or bracken-clad slopes which characterize the fell country. Only in the last two centuries has tree-planting around the lakes, the southern valleys, and, more recently, larger-scale forestry and the planting of conifers, begun to re-clothe the region.

Within the national park there is a quite remarkable range of habitat, from sand dunes on the coast to the highest mountains in England, and this is reflected in the interesting animal and plant life of the area. The nature reserve at Ravenglass Dunes is the home of the largest breeding colony of black-headed gulls in England, while on the highest slopes of the fells such mountain plants as alpine lady's mantle and saxifrage are to be found. On the fells, too, are found red deer. The herd roaming the high land around Martindale,

Mosedale and the approach to Black Sail Pass.

Wastwater, with the famous screes on the right. In the background (centre) is Great Gable.

in the eastern part of the park, is believed to be one of the few remaining sur-
vivals of the native wild stock. Reafforestation has increased the numbers of
rabbits, hares, the foxes that prey upon them, and of roe deer, which, though
not the forester's best friend, certainly help to make the forests more attractive
to visitors. The forest museum at Grizedale, and the trails that start from it, are
a good introduction to the rich woodland fauna of the park.

Sheep are the basis of the agricultural economy of much of the park. Hill
grazing land goes up to all but the highest summits, though often it will carry
no more than one sheep per acre. The sheep-runs may be enormous, separated
from each other and from the lower pastures, or 'in-by' land, by the rough dry-
stone walls which are such a feature of the national park. But the mountain
breeds, such as the local Herdwick, a small sheep with a pale face and dark,
rusty brown fleece, have the useful characteristic of returning to their heaf, or
native hill pasture, and do not normally stray long distances.

Of the national park's other industries, mining has a considerable past but
a doubtful future. The pockets of lead, copper and, in the south, iron ore were
widespread but never large enough to support mining on a massive scale. A
more unusual mineral, graphite, was mined in Borrowdale until it gave out,
though Keswick still retains its pencil industry as a legacy. Quarrying is more
important nowadays; besides the volcanic rocks used for roadmetal, there are
the granites of Shap, still a popular facing material for buildings, and the
handsome blue and green slates of Broughton Moors and Honister, used

Striding Edge, Helvellyn, a stern test in winter conditions.

mainly for floors and walls in such impressive modern buildings as Coventry Cathedral. The lakes, fed by high rainfall in the hills, are valuable in water supply, particularly to Manchester, which owns two, Thirlmere and Hawes-water, and abstracts from others.

But the industry with the greatest potential for growth is undoubtedly the holiday industry. The pressure comes in all forms: more caravan parks are needed, more new hotels and rented accommodation. Boats arrive by the score, by road, and they too need accommodation. Arguments are put forward for cinemas and theatres (and why not a casino on Windermere? a Frenchman once asked me). To cope with this pressure, these demands, is the most acute problem of the national park authority. How much development to permit, and of what sort, within a landscape as intimate and easily spoilt as that of the Lake District, is a matter of constant argument. Only one thing is certain: more and more people will want to come to the Lake District, and in their wake will come the applications from those wishing to cater for, and profit from, the numbers.

To appreciate why the Lake District has this attraction for so many, it is worth looking back a century or two at what people have visited the area for. It was best avoided altogether 250 years ago. 'This part of the country yields little or nothing at all', wrote merchant-minded Defoe; the hills 'had an un-hospitable terror in them' and 'all the pleasant part of England was at an end'. But by the end of the eighteenth century terror had given way to romantic fascination. William Gilpin, philosopher of the picturesque, was himself a Cumbrian, and Wordsworth, even before bringing out his guidebook in 1835, had done as much as anyone to make the region and its beauty a public property. True, the old man grumbled at the coming of the railway to Windermere, and perhaps felt that inspiration was dented by being so avail-able, but over the years many people who have visited and returned to the Lake District have done so because of a picture they have in their minds. This picture is compounded of the reflections of mountains in a lake surface, changes of light and shade on the fells, peace, solitude, a certain quality in the air, and emotions that, back in the town or city, they will be able to recollect in tranquillity.

But the national park is also visited for the open-air recreation it offers, the walking, climbing, riding, sailing on the lakes, skating and skiing in winter. Much of the park is ill-suited to the organized tour or sightseeing, being less than conveniently served with roads. Nor has it the sort of attrac-tions best appreciated in a crowd, so that catering for masses of people is seldom appropriate and may serve only to draw into the park more people than it can reasonably accommodate, unless developments are carefully related to an overall plan of management.

For all that is written about the Lake District bursting at the seams, though,

Stang End Farm, Little Langdale, whitewashed, slate-roofed and set in the hillside.

View down the Kirkstone Pass to Brothers Water. Over the crags in the background lies Martindale Forest.

the national park is a large area and it is still possible, even during the holiday season, to escape one's neighbours within its boundaries, while those visiting the park in spring or autumn, or during the winter months, will find it as beautiful and very much quieter. A longer season and greater dispersal throughout the area of the park could undoubtedly cope with the increasing number of visitors for many years to come.

There is indeed so much to do and so much to see in the national park that it is really a pity to see any part of it over-used. It is one of the aims of the park's information service, and of the national park centre at Brockhole, Windermere, to relieve the strain on the well-known beauty spots by fitting them into the context of the whole park and by awakening new interests in the visitor. Curiosity about the relics of the past to be found in the park might take him to see two fine stone circles as far apart as Castlerigg, near Keswick, and Swinside, in the rolling country just west of the Duddon Valley, or to follow the route the Romans used from Ambleside to their impressively sited fort near the summit of Hardknott Pass and on down Eskdale to their port at

64

I.   Lake District National Park: Grasmere.

Silecroft Beaches, on the park's short coastline, with Black Combe rising in the background.

Ravenglass. Or again, to visit the quiet ruins of Calder Abbey or the fine tower of Shap Abbey, respectively at the western and eastern edges of the park. An interest in the Lake District's famous literary figures could go well beyond a visit to Wordsworth's cottage and the museum by Grasmere. Besides following up the Wordsworth trail to the much less visited Rydal Mount and to the elegant house in Cockermouth which the young poet unfortunately had to quit for more humble quarters in Penrith, there could be a pilgrimage to Brantwood, Ruskin's handsome house overlooking Coniston Water, or to the Ruskin Museum in Coniston village across the lake. Or younger readers might spend a delightful day in identifying the scenes in and around Beatrix Potter's home at Sawrey, where this remarkable woman constructed her series of stories based on the animals, both wild and tame, of her acquaintance. Lectures, leaflets and an exhibition at the national park centre help to answer some of the initial questions, but the emphasis is always on getting people to go and see for themselves the full richness of the park.

This richness is such that holiday visitors to the park would do well to

The Herdwick sheep, a native breed accustomed to the rough fell grazing.

regard it as a number of distinct areas each with its centres of accommodation, and mountains and passes to explore. Thus Windermere, Ambleside and Coniston serve their lake areas and also the southern routes into the Central Fells; Glenridding and Patterdale are well placed for the Helvellyn range to the west and also for the nearer of the remote Eastern Fells. Borrowdale presents a whole series of different ways into the Central Fells, while Keswick also looks north to the Skiddaw and Saddleback slopes and west to the Derwent Fells. To stay in the western dales, in Eskdale or the Duddon Valley where there are no large centres of accommodation gives yet another approach, while the southern towns, both in and just outside the park, like Broughton-in-Furness, Millom and Ulverston, all have their advantages. Kendal, in the south-east, also has claims as a park touring centre; the River Kent which runs through Kendal drains the valleys of Kentmere and Longsleddale which both reach up into the Eastern Fells.

Although outside the park boundary, Kendal is in fact the administrative centre, headquarters of the Lake District Planning Board. Members of the Board are appointed by the three counties of Cumberland, Westmorland and Lancashire, which also serve the Board through their Planning Officers, and the Clerk is the Clerk of Westmorland County Council. The park symbol is based on the well known view of Great Gable from Wasdale.

CENTRES   Ambleside, Broughton in Furness, Cockermouth, Glenridding/Patterdale, Grange-over-Sands, Kendal, Keswick, Grasmere, Penrith, Windermere/Bowness

PLACES OF INTEREST   Aira Force, Brantwood, Brockhole (National Park Centre), Calder Abbey, Castlerigg Stone Circle, Crosthwaite Church, Dove Cottage, Grizedale, Hardknott (Roman fort), Hawkshead (church, courthouse, grammar school), Hill Top (Sawrey), Lodore Falls, Lowther Park, Muncaster Castle, Ravenglass, Rydal Mount, Scale Force (Buttermere), Shap Abbey, Shoulthwaite Fort (Thirlmere), Swinside Stone Circle, Townend (Troutbeck)

North York Moors

In 1952 an area of 553 square miles of the North Riding of Yorkshire became the country's sixth national park. The name is something of a mistake: the greater part of the park is made up of an area more commonly known as the Yorkshire Moors (at nearest some twenty-five miles from the city of York) and the earlier reports had referred to it more correctly as the North Yorkshire Moors. But if its nomenclature is uncertain, geographically this is one of the best defined of the national parks. Over much of its length the park boundary coincides with the edge of a high moorland plateau, often abrupt and ramparted. On the north the Cleveland escarpment overlooks busy, expanding Teesside, on the west and south-west are the Hambleton Hills rising steeply from the Vale of York, to the south a more uneven boundary runs through the towns and villages of the moor edge above the broad Vale of Pickering, and to east and north-east lies the sea.

The heart of the park is the great expanse of heather moor, the largest in the country. Known in the past as Blackamoor, it is indeed brown-black and sinister for much of the year, but in late August it becomes a glorious green and purple sea. Rich and subtle colouring is a characteristic of this landscape and of its native buildings, the dark gold sandstone farmhouses and cottages with their crisp white window-frames and red pantile roofs. From east to west the moors stretch for over thirty miles, with hardly a road crossing them in this direction, for the main dales run north and south and the few ways through the area either follow these deep trenches or run along the lofty ridges between. The southern and western parts of the moors and the dales as far east as Rosedale are sometimes included in the general name Ryedale. Together with the Hambleton and Cleveland Hills, the Tabular Hills north-west of Scarborough and the coastal belt, they provide, within the one upland block of land, as wide a range of scenery as could be found in any national park.

The cliffs of the park's fine coastline give a good section through the vast thickness of Jurassic rocks on which the landscape of the park is based. In any of the broader bays along the coast these rocks can be seen dipping gently from north to south, so that one looks for the oldest rocks at the foot of Boulby Cliff or where a slight upward warping of the strata has allowed the sea to cut back semicircular bays. The dark clays and shales from the base of the Jurassic system are in fact best seen in the long curved 'scars' exposed at low tide in Robin Hood's Bay. Moving upwards, the later rocks include the

The western approach to the park; Gormire Lake and Sutton Bank.

Cleveland Ironstone, the Alum Shales and the Jet Rock, all worked at various times along the coast, as can be seen in the excavated headland of Kettleness and the tiny ironstone-loading harbour of Port Mulgrave. Next comes a series of silts and sandstones known as the Estuarine Series and best seen at Hayburn Wyke or Cloughton Wyke. These rocks, laid down in estuary or delta conditions millions of years ago, are the basis of the park's moorland; they cover almost the whole central area of the park except where the deeper dales have cut through to the rocks beneath. The youngest rocks in the park, from the Upper Jurassic, do not reach the coastline within its boundaries, but form Castle Hill at Scarborough, the scarp of the Tabular Hills inland, the southern fringes of the park, and the Hambleton Hills. They are mainly light-coloured limestones, quarried for lime and as a building stone, in which form they contribute to the attractive appearance of the villages and stone walls of the country between Scarborough and Helmsley.

The gentle folding that was noticeable at Robin Hood's Bay was part of a system of earth movements which warped the tilted platform of rocks making

Bilsdale, looking north, before the prominent television mast was put up.

up the park. To take the ridge road from Hutton-le-Hole to Castleton leads one over the centre of the Cleveland Dome. This was the main such movement and was responsible for the pattern of rivers draining south and north. But the nature of their valleys, as well as much of the landscape around the park's edges, also owe much to the action of ice. As the Ice Age drew to a close, large lakes developed in Eskdale and the Vale of Pickering, dammed up by the great North Sea ice sheet. The almost riverless Newtondale is an overflow channel scoured out by meltwaters between the two lakes, and the whole of the coastal belt's mixed farming land results from the cover of boulder clay left by the ice.

The park's more recent history begins with the huge assembly of cairns and burial mounds, mostly of the Bronze Age. So numerous are these in

Ralph Cross, at the summit of one of the long, dark moorland ridges. The hollow at the top of the shaft is for alms.

The surprise view of Farndale, Gillamoor.

most parts of the moors that the Scheduled List of the Department of the Environment can give over a hundred locations, many with large groups of barrows. Walkers on the Cleveland Way or the Lyke Wake Walk (see p. 209) can hardly fail to be aware of these ancient monuments and the named 'howes' or cairns on the highest ground that so often form their only land-marks. Not that the wastes are trackless, for the moors are crossed by paths and 'trods' of all ages, used by shepherds, jet miners, smugglers, and probably also by the hobs and witches that are notorious in this part of Yorkshire. One of the most remarkable routes is the Roman road that runs north from the half-hidden old camp at Cawthorn, three miles from Pickering. At its best bet-ween Stape and Wheeldale, where a length has been exposed, it can be seen as a 15-foot carriageway, properly drained with gutters and culverts. The road may well have linked with the signal stations at Huntcliff, Goldsborough and Ravenscar that kept watch for Saxon invaders in the fourth century.

72

Farndale daffodils.

Not far from the line of the road, near Stape, stands Mauley Cross, a good example of the stone crosses that are such familiar features to all who travel the moors. One of the best-known is the 9-foot Ralph Cross at the summit of the Blakey Rigg–Castleton Rigg road; another is Lilla Cross on Fylingdales Moor, dating from around 626 and reputedly the oldest Christian cross in the North.

Many of the moorland crosses are mediaeval and may well have served as waymarks for visitors to and from the great monasteries of this region. The abbeys of Rievaulx and Byland are among the finest monastic ruins in the North. Byland was once an even closer neighbour of Rievaulx, the earlier foundation by a dozen years in 1131, but its original site on the Rye near Old Byland was so close that the two houses could hear each other's bells, and the younger house eventually moved over the moors to the foot of Wass Bank, though it retained its first name. The classic view of Rievaulx, tucked into

Levisham Station in narrow Newtondale. Stephenson's railway is now closed but a steam train service is to be restored by railway enthusiasts.

the steep-sided valley of the Rye, is from the Terrace, a long strip of lawn put in by Thomas Duncombe along the valley brow in the eighteenth century as part of the landscape gardening of Duncombe Park. A very different monastery is to be found at the foot of the Cleveland Hills near Osmotherley: Mount Grace Priory is a house of the hermit-like Carthusians whose individual cells surround a huge cloister 230 feet across.

Rievaulx and Byland, with Gisborough, had business interests in many parts of the moors, establishing the sheep farming pattern and exploiting the iron ores in Bilsdale, Rosedale and Glaisdale. Wood for charcoal used in the furnaces was taken in large quantities from the surrounding forests, and this, together with clearance for farming, largely produced the moorland appearance we see today. Farming nowadays is still based on sheep for the higher farms, but there are prosperous dairy farms in the dales, and in some places the plough is claiming back parts of the moor. Forestry is putting back the trees

Wade's Causeway, the Roman Road over Wheeldale Moor, south-west of Goathland.

in some areas, pine and larch being the commonest planted. Much of Allerston Forest is now well grown enough to make the Forestry Commission's scenic drive from Dalby to Hackness a very popular attraction.

The mining in Cleveland declined after reaching its peak in the last century, when iron, alum and jet were all actively sought. Alum-working scars are slow to heal, but the main effects of iron working lie outside the park's northern boundary. Today's interest in what lies under the park centres on natural gas and potash. Though there are some productive wellheads for gas in the park north of Pickering, they are fairly unobtrusively sited in forest clearings. When proposals were entered to look for gas on the exposed northern edge of the moors at Stoney Ridge, these were turned down by the Secretary of State for the Environment. But applications to exploit potash which had been found at great depth under the coastal areas of the park had already been given, no fewer than three large companies planning to mine the deposits.

A terrace of stone cottages with their pantile roofs, Thornton-le-Dale.

In the event only one of the mines has gone ahead, that at Boulby, in the north-east corner of the park, and here conditions were imposed on the treatment of waste and the discharge of effluent to the sea.

The park's other main problems have been over military installations and reservoirs. The decision to erect the Early Warning System for missiles at Fylingdales in 1960 was greeted with some dismay, though it is fair to say that the 'golf ball' radomes now have their admirers. On the positive side an end to artillery practice in the same area enabled Lilla Cross, which had been removed for safety to Sil Howe near the Whitby-Pickering road, to return to Lilla Howe. On the water front, a reservoir in Farndale, famous for its miles of wild daffodils, had long been a threat, but in 1971 a private Bill to promote the scheme was rejected by Parliament.

The Peak, Ravenscar. The huge fault in the rocks can be clearly seen, following the line of the track from beach to cliff top.

Farndale is a local nature reserve, and in Spring the park's warden and his voluntary helpers establish a centre in the valley to cope with the flood of visitors that fills the narrow roads, but there is much of natural history interest in other parts of the park as well. A field museum has been set up by the Forestry Commission at Midge Hall near to the famous waterfall of Falling Foss, and in the limestone country, notable for its rich flora, there is a nature trail at Sutton Bank. On the coast another nature trail descends to the beach from Ravenscar, 600 feet above Robin Hood's Bay, where the principal interest is geological.

Many who visit the North Yorkshire coast are familiar only with the resorts and the bays to which there is road access. But the best way to see the splendours of the park's cliff scenery is on foot, and here the Cleveland Way (see p. 209) provides a path along the whole park coastline. Whitby and Scarborough, both just outside the park, are good centres for exploring the coastal belt, though the smaller settlements of Robin Hood's Bay, Runswick Bay and Staithes also have accommodation. For the southern fringe of the park Pickering, and for Ryedale and the Hambletons Helmsley, are good choices. Goathland makes a good inland centre for walking, and for the Cleveland Hills there are the market towns of Stokesley and Guisborough between the park and Teesside.

The whole of the park area falling within the North Riding of Yorkshire, the planning authority is a committee of North Riding County Council, whose offices are at Northallerton. The park symbol, like that of the Yorkshire Dales, is the white rose of York.

CENTRES Helmsley, Middlesbrough, Northallerton, Pickering, Saltburn, Scarborough, Whitby

PLACES OF INTEREST Allerston Forest Drive, Boulby Cliff, Bridestones (Staindale), Byland Abbey, Coxwold, Duncombe Park, Easby Moor (Cook Monument), Falling Foss (trail), Farndale, Forge Valley, Goathland, Gormire Lake, Helmsley Castle, Hole of Horcum, Hutton-le-Hole (Folk Museum), Lastingham, Mount Grace Priory, Mulgrave Castle, Ralph Cross, Ravenscar (trail), Rievaulx Abbey, Robin Hood's Bay, Roseberry Topping, Runswick Bay, Staithes, Sutton Bank (trail), Thornton Dale, Wade's Causeway (Roman road), Whitby Abbey

Northumberland

The first suggestions for a national park in Northumberland specified the Roman Wall area, but in 1954 the National Parks Commission, whose members had visited and been impressed by the Cheviot country, proposed a Cheviot National Park. While welcoming the proposal the County Council advised the Commission to consider a much larger park which would include a stretch of the Roman Wall, the intervening moorlands and the Kielder Forest; so the Commission revisited the area, also starting discussions with the Forestry Commission. The result was a national park of 398 square miles designated in 1955 extending from the Wall to the Border country, while the Forestry Commission simultaneously created the adjoining Border Forest Park of some 175 square miles, including not only Kielder Forest but the neighbour forests of Kershope, Newcastleton and Wauchope.

As this history suggests, the park falls naturally into a number of regions. Together they make up the greater part of the county's open hill country, but each has its own distinct characteristics. In the north are the Cheviot Hills, the largest of these regions, extending south as far as Coquetdale. The Simonside Hills, an eastward-curving arc, and Coquetdale itself form the second region, and the valleys of Redesdale and the North Tyne the third and fourth. In the south the Roman Wall area makes a fifth distinct region.

The underlying rocks reflect the landscape differences of these regions of the park. The Cheviot (2676 feet) is the domed centre of an old volcano which, millions of years ago, spewed out rock debris and lava over the surrounding area, and which, later, was invaded from below by a molten granite mass. The area of the granite at the surface is roughly marked out by the extent of heather, which likes the acid soils derived from the granite. Around the Cheviot the rocks dip away to east and south, and the next striking feature is the ridge of Fell Sandstone that forms the Simonside Hills. Redesdale and the North Tyne Valley cut into the softer shales of the next series of rocks, and there is a softer, more wooded appearance to the landscape, though harder sandstone bands again produce some higher heather-clad ground. The Roman Wall country is dominated by the Whin Sill, its hard basalt giving the line of crags along which the Wall runs. The movement of ice over this area scooped out the shales beneath the crags and made the hollows now filled by Crag Lough, Greenlee Lough and Broomlee Lough.

To the physical beauty of the countryside of this national park another dimension is added in the interest of its history. It is an area where awareness

Roman Wall country; the view near Walltown Crags.

of the past comes easily, where little has changed over centuries and where the same wide horizons and distant views must have been available to Roman legions, Pictish tribesmen, missionary saints, moss-troopers, smugglers and drovers.

II.   Peak District National Park: the view over Castleton from Peveril Castle.

Cheviot country; the Harthope Valley looking towards Hedgehope.

Yeavering Bell, in the north of the park where the steep slopes of the Cheviot Hills stand above the valley of the Till, has on its summit a hill-fort and settlement of colossal size, thirteen acres in extent and containing traces of some 130 huts. Many more camps and walled settlements are to be

The fourteenth-century pele tower which forms part of the rectory at Elsdon.

found in this Cheviot area, but they probably stood less in need of fortification after the growth of Roman control removed the need for this security. The Romano-British village of Greaves Ash, up the Breamish valley from Ingram, shows hut remains straddling earlier fortifications. Roman military activity did not stop short at the Wall; north from Corbridge into Scotland ran Dere

Linhope Spout, at the head of the Breamish Valley.

Street, crossing the park via Redesdale where it links three outlying forts at Risingham, Elishaw and High Rochester. There is also a series of marching camps at Chew Green near the head of the Coquet, best seen from Harden Edge.

The Breamish Valley is popular with visitors to the park, and the park authority has negotiated an agreement with the landowner giving access to the public.

But it is the Wall that most forcibly demonstrates the power and the organization of Ancient Rome. The fifteen miles of the Wall within the park include the best preserved section of this unique monument, as well as forts, milecastles, milestones, temples and bath-houses. Approaching from Newcastle along the Military Road, past the camps at Chesters and Carrawburgh, where there are the remains of a temple to Mithras, one sees the Wall snaking along over the crags half a mile to the north. The fort of Housesteads, perhaps

84

The North Gate at Housesteads, most impressive of the Roman forts on the Wall.

the most striking of the wall-forts, lies within this stretch. The Wall, its associated ditches, and the road constituted a military zone, along which troops could be moved and against which attackers could be pinned down. The presence of the formidable Vallum ditch south of the road indicates that there could be raiders from either side. So little has changed in the surrounding areas that it is not difficult to recapture the spirit of the watch, looking out from the wall on its crags to the open moors. Perhaps the most time-arresting sight of all is an uncompleted milecastle and ditch at the eastern end of the stretch within the park; here can be seen the blocks of Whin Sill rock left for splitting up, and the holes into which the Romans drove their wedges.

When the Anglo-Saxon kingdom of Northumbria was a power holding tribute from kingdoms to the south, King Edwin (founder of Edinburgh), who had an extensive palace just outside the park's northern boundary, was converted to Christianity by St Paulinus. For thirty-six days, Bede records, Paulinus stayed at Yeavering instructing the Northumbrians and baptizing them in the River Glen. Later missions to the area included those of St Aidan

and St Cuthbert from Lindisfarne on the coast. Today, one of the most interesting church treasures in this region is the mediaeval relief sculpture in Kirknewton church with its three kilted Wise Men offering their gifts to a
robust-looking infant Christ.

From mediaeval times the central Border regions of the park claim attention. This is the land of the Border ballads, of Chevy Chase and the Battle
of Otterburn (1388), the site of which is marked by the Percy Cross just outside the village on the road to Scotland. It is also the land of the Border raiders
and outlaws against whose attacks the fortified towers and pele-houses were
built. A good example can be seen at Elsdon, where the rectory is a solid-looking
pele tower with walls 8 feet thick. Although Redesdale formed, as it does
today, a main route into Scotland, it was for long a perilous route, for this
area and North Tynedale were also the haunt of the moss-trooper and the
reiver. So notorious was it that a sixteenth-century Newcastle byelaw against
the taking of apprentices born in either of these two valleys was not repealed
until 1771. Besides the road over Redeswire, site of the last serious Border
affray in 1575, there are the other roads into Scotland used by the drovers who
came south from the big fairs at Falkirk with their herds of black cattle for the
English markets. Some went by Falstone on the North Tyne from Hawick,
others by Clennell Street, a green ridge road over the Cheviots from Yetholm
on the Bowmont Water to Alwinton on the Coquet.

Alwinton and Yetholm Shows in early October, and also those at Falstone
in August and Ingram and Rochester in September, are important events
in the park, where sheep farming and forestry are the main occupations.
Nearly three-quarters of the park area is classified as rough grazing, and there
is a total sheep population in summer of around a quarter of a million. Besides
the distinctive Cheviot breeds with their white faces and pricked up ears,
Swaledales and, particularly on the highest land, the Scottish Blackface sheep
are common. Hill farming is a hard life, with little time for relaxation, but
local sport still thrives, particularly hunting and beagling. There are some
nine packs which hunt in and around the park, the Cheviot Hills especially
providing some fine long runs. Fishing in rivers in and near the park is
generally private, but facilities for visitors are offered by some hotels and local
clubs. Some of the cheapest salmon fishing in the country is obtainable on the
Coquet.

Much of the park is ideal riding country and the increasingly popular
sport of pony trekking, with stables in the Breamish, Coquet and Tyne
valleys, offers an excellent way of following the hill routes. Two locations that
attract rock climbers are the sandstone edges of the Simonside Hills and the
cliffs of the Whin Sill at Crag Lough. For walkers there is a vast acreage of
open country over which, without formal access agreements, access has
traditionally been permitted, subject to walkers avoiding disturbance to game

86

Climbers on the rocks of the Whin Sill above Crag Lough.

and livestock. Fine walking routes are too numerous to mention, but many visitors to the park will want to reach the summit of the Cheviot, most commonly approached by the valley of the Harthope Burn, or to follow the dramatic central section of the Wall from Sewing Shields to Thirlwall. Others will want to seek out the waterfalls of Linhope Spout, reached from Ingram on the way to the summit of Hedgehope, Davidson's Linn on the Usway Burn just above the site of Rory's Still, a former illicit whisky distillery, or the Seven Linns on the Chirdon Burn in the North Tyne Valley. The sight of a salmon leaping against the rapids on these fast-flowing streams, or of the wild goats that inhabit the remoter parts of the Cheviot region, are added attractions not only for those with an interest in natural history. But there is much too for the naturalist, for the park has a rich diversity of plant and animal life. The one nature reserve in the park has more of a specialist interest, being one of the best examples of actively growing blanket bog. The Northumberland and Durham Naturalists' Trust was one of the first to organize popular nature trails, some of them within the bounds of the park.

Only in the centre of the park is there any major obstacle to the walker: this is the Redesdale All Arms Range. The Roman cohorts who operated the artillery base of Bremenium (High Rochester), with its *ballistae* for hurling stones, would no doubt have approved of the modern camp at nearby Otterburn and the extensive training area to the north, but it does not sit well in a national park. Warning notices show where there is safe access, red flags are flown in firing areas, and advance times of firing can be obtained from the camp or from notices at local Post Offices.

The Planning Committee of the national park is a separate committee of Northumberland County Council, which is the planning authority. There are three park information centres: at Ingram in the Breamish Valley, serving the Cheviot region; at Byrness in Redesdale, on the only main road through the park, the A68; and at Once Brewed, on the Military Road (B6318), north-west of Bardon Mill. The last two stand not far from the line of the Pennine Way (see p. 223), which threads its way through the park from Greenhead on the Wall to the Cheviot and on down to Kirk Yetholm over the Border. The Northumberland park sign, perhaps the most attractive of the nine, is a silhouette of that familiar bird of the moorland, the curlew.

CENTRES   Hexham, Newcastle upon Tyne, Otterburn, Rothbury, Wooler

PLACES OF INTEREST   Alwinton, Chesterholm, Chew Green (Roman forts), College Valley, Crag Lough, Elsdon, Greaves Ash (prehistoric village), Hadrian's Wall (and forts at Housesteads, Carrawburgh), Harbottle, Holystone, Ingram, Kirknewton, Linhope Spout, Nine Nicks of Thirlwall, Rochester (Bremenium fort), Yeavering Bell

Peak District

Manchester and Sheffield lie on either side, separated by the sombre moorlands that merge into the southern end of the Pennines. To the north is the industrial West Riding of Yorkshire; to the south, Derby, Nottingham and the Midlands; and to the west, the busy towns of the Cheshire Plain. It does not seem a promising place to establish Britain's first national park. But it is the Peak District that holds this distinction, and holds it proudly. Its record as a protected landscape won it a Conservation Diploma of the Council of Europe in 1966, an award it still holds. The 542-square-mile national park was designated in 1950 and began to operate the following year. It covers a remarkably rich and varied area of hills, expanses of moorland, steep-sided dales and broad winding valleys, where the changing contours make it easy to forget that this is a park more densely populated and more visited than any other.

There is no peak to the Peak District; the origins of the name are ascribed by some to pig-keeping in former times, by others to early tribes inhabiting the area. But the basic structure is, like that of the Pennines, a broad uplifted and elongated dome, worn away in the centre. The youngest rock thus exposed is the grey limestone of the southern part of the park, a region sometimes referred to as the 'White Peak' with the characteristic landscape of light and subtle green and grey colouring. A network of limestone walls separates large, thinly grassed pastures on the uplands, and the upper reaches of the valleys are often dry, the water having sunk underground to reappear as a clear stream in the narrow, wooded, lower dales.

At the edges of this limestone region there are broader valleys, greener and more wooded, cut in the shales which form part of the next series of rocks. Sandstones and thin grits also form part of this series, a great thickness of which can be seen in the face of Mam Tor, sometimes known as the 'Shivering Mountain' because of the unstable nature of this vast cliff. To the east and west the flanks of the peak dome are defined by the long, dark gritstone edges which are such a feature of the Peak District and so popular with climbers. The Millstone Grit which forms these scarps dips away on either side of the park to disappear under the younger Coal Measures, but in the northern part of the park are the huge gritstone plateaux of Kinder, Bleaklow and Black Hill, with expanses of peat carved by the elements into a weird pattern of 'groughs'.

Nab End, looking across upper Dovedale from Hitter Hill near Earl Sterndale.

The quarrying of limestone is the most important industry of the area, but of the several million tons extracted annually most is won in the area around Buxton, which was excluded from the park for this reason, and south of Matlock, again outside the park boundary. Where limestone and shale occur side by side, as at the edge of the Hope Valley, cement can be made. The huge cement works at Bradwell is the largest enterprise in the park. Associated with the limestone and injected into it at the time of the uplifting of the dome are valuable minerals, including lead ore, barytes and fluorspar. Lead was one of the first attractions of the area, and its mining has a long history. Defoe witnessed a lead miner appearing from one of the 'grooves': 'the man was a most uncouth spectacle; he was clothed all in leather, had a cap of the same without brims, some tools in a little basket which he drew up with him . . . he was lean as a skeleton, pale as a dead corpse, his hair and beard a deep black, his flesh lank, and, as we thought, something of the colour of the lead itself.' Nowadays it is the other two minerals that are more important, and the tips of the

The lip of the Kinder plateau at Kinder Downfall, seen here in dry weather; after heavy rain there is a spectacular 100-foot waterfall.

old lead mines are worked over for fluorspar discarded as useless in earlier days. Near Castleton the beautiful variety of fluorspar known as Blue John occurs at Treak Cliff, and ornaments made from it can be seen in the shops.

Lead mining activity has obscured some of the sites of earthworks and other prehistoric remains in the limestone areas of the park, but it is still evident that from the New Stone Age onwards the sparsely wooded uplands

Lathkill Dale, one of the many pleasant limestone valleys in the southern part of the park.

attracted settlers. One of the finest monuments in the park is the stone circle within earthworks at Arbor Low, 250 feet across and ascribed to the Beaker Folk of 3,800 years ago. Bronze Age monuments are found more commonly on the gritstone moorlands, as at Stanton Moor above Darley Dale, while there are several Iron Age forts with contoured defences, notably the one at Mam Tor. At Brough there are remains of a Roman fort, and Roman roads

The impressive profile of Back Tor, near Castleton.

centred on this and on Buxton, where the hot springs were known, strike straight across the uplands of the park. From Saxon times, there are carved crosses at Bakewell, Bradbourne, Eyam, Hope, Ilam, and several other places.

The Norman castle of the Peak perched above Castleton forms the emblem of the national park. It is a ruin particularly impressive because of its site; established by William Peveril and rebuilt in the twelfth century, the date of the keep, it was never lived in for long and fell out of use in the sixteenth century. What Peak Castle might have become given a more accommodating site can be seen at Haddon Hall. Built on a bluff overlooking the River Wye, this is a fascinating house architecturally, built around two courtyards and revealing its growth from a mediaeval to a Jacobean manor. It has been owned by only two families, the Vernons and the Manners, now Dukes of Rutland. The intimate terraced gardens of Haddon, clinging to their steep slopes, are in complete contrast to the park and gardens of the other great

Water crowfoot in Dovedale.

house in the neighbouring valley of the Derwent. The grounds of Chatsworth House were conceived on the grandest of scales. In the eighteenth and nineteenth centuries 'Capability' Brown under the fourth Duke of Devonshire and Paxton under the sixth Duke were amongst the architects, adding landscaping effects to the classical grandeur of the first Duke's garden. After these splendid grounds, with the Great Cascade, canals, fountains and distant

The spectacular dry gorge of The Winnats just west of Castleton.

groups of trees, the house itself seems cluttered; priceless treasures stand cheek by jowl with tasteless gifts and purchases so that the overall impression is one of magnificent vulgarity.

Another fine park is that at Lyme Hall, the third great house of the Peak District, owned by the National Trust and managed by Stockport Corporation. But there are also many smaller houses of great interest, like the group around Hathersage built by the Eyre family in such a way, it is said, that the sons' houses were hidden from each other but not from their father's house. High-low, Offerton and North Lees Halls are part of this group, the last of which has been identified by some as the 'Thornfield Hall' of Charlotte Brontë's *Jane Eyre*.

A particularly apt theme for a characteristic well dressing at the village of Tissington, no great distance from Dovedale.

Up to the time when Charlotte Brontë was visiting friends in Hathersage, the Peak District had been an isolated place. But though the Industrial Revolution brought communications up the dales and over the moors, the villages retained much of their individuality and many of their old customs. That of well-dressing is probably the best known, originally practised at Tissington's five wells but also to be seen at Ashford-in-the-Water, Eyam, Tideswell,

III.   Pembrokeshire Coast National Park: Stackpole Quay.

Fishing in the Dove; in the background is Thorpe Cloud.

Youlgreave, Hope and other villages. The elaborate pictures are made up of flowers, leaves and other natural objects pressed into a matrix of soft clay. Tradition has it that wells were first dressed as a thanksgiving for escape from the Black Death in the fourteenth century. The village of Eyam (pronounced as in 'stream') was less fortunate in 1665, when the Great Plague wiped out all but a sixth of its inhabitants, who heroically imposed quarantine on themselves.

The Peak is the most densely populated national park; some 40,000 people live within its boundaries. While there is much commuting, particularly into

Sheffield, many people are employed in the park itself—in farming, in the quarrying and mineral industries, and in light manufacturing industry. Farming is mostly dairy or, especially in the north of the park, sheep. Here there are large areas of heather moor, which serve as rough grazing, grouse moors, water gathering grounds, and, in recent years, for open-air recreation.

Public access to the gritstone moorlands of the Peak District has had a stormy history, for no tradition of free access, as in the Lake District, existed here. The park planning authority made one of its earliest jobs the negotiation of access agreements with local landowners, with whose co-operation nearly seventy-four square miles of open country are now available to the public. Notices indicating the areas over which such agreements exist are displayed on footpaths and other approaches, and at weekends and holiday times national park wardens, including part-timers and volunteers, help to see that access bye-laws are observed.

Walking is popular in the Peak, where most of the visitors are there for the day or the half day. The park gets over ten million visitors a year, and $17\frac{1}{2}$ million people live within fifty miles of the boundaries, so that numbers are only likely to increase. In a few minutes you can be out of the city of Sheffield and heading over moorland to the gritstone edges. This means that at times traffic can be heavy up and down the rocks of Stanage Edge, for instance, as well as on the park's approach roads.

One of the park's pressing problems is the fact that most visitors now come by car instead of by bus and train, as in the past. But the Peak has a better road network than most of the other parks, with some fine high-level routes and viewpoints for motorists, so that they do not always want to leave their cars. Over fifty lay-bys, together with larger car parks in the more popular places, have been provided since designation, and the park authority produces a special motorists' map. Narrow roads and weekend congestion sometimes need special treatment, however, and for this reason an experiment was carried out by the park authority and the Countryside Commission. It involved the closure of four miles of road on summer weekends and holidays in the upper Goyt Valley in 1970 and 1971. Car parks were established at the edge of the motorless zone, with a minibus service to run between them, also picnic sites, marked footpaths and a nature trail in the valley itself. People could again walk, cycle or wheel pushchairs along the roads into the valley. This positive approach to a knotty problem disarmed much of the initial suspicion and hostility; besides providing some useful practical information on what can and cannot be done, the Goyt Valley Experiment has done a lot to change people's attitudes to the need for some sort of traffic management in popular parts of the countryside.

As an upland area close to centres of population, the park has another problem in the constant pressure for new sites for reservoirs. There are already

Climbing on the gritstone of Stanage Edge.

fifty-five reservoirs, each of more than four acres in extent, within the park, and another thirty-six within two miles of its boundaries, but the investigation of potential sites goes on. The installation of filtration plants these days avoids the barring of the gathering grounds of reservoirs to public access, but the area under water is still rendered unavailable, and it is depressing that so few of the larger reservoirs allow recreation on the water. Where they do, the demand for sailing facilities outstrips the supply.

The national park authority is the Peak Park Planning Board, which was formed in 1951. On it are represented the five local authority planning interests—Derbyshire, Staffordshire, Cheshire and West Riding County Councils, and Sheffield County Borough Council. The Board has its own Director, staff and offices, and operates from Aldern House on the outskirts of Bakewell. Mention has been made of some of the work of the authority; amongst other activities the information services, woodlands policy and restoration schemes are important. The Board has information centres at Bakewell, Buxton, Castleton and Edale at which a wide range of leaflets and publications are available free and for sale. Over 350 acres of woodland are managed by the Board in this landscape where groups of trees can be particularly vital; a group regeneration system is operated with around 20,000 trees a year being planted. Finally, mention should be made of the $11\frac{1}{2}$-mile Tissington Trail between Hartington and Mapleton. This section of the disused Ashbourne-Buxton railway line was bought, cleared and planted as a green track for hikers and horse riders, with picnic places and access car parks. It opened in 1971 and is the first of a number of such scenic ex-railway routes contemplated by the Board.

CENTRES   Ashbourne, Bakewell, Buxton, Manchester, Matlock, Sheffield, Stockport

PLACES OF INTEREST   Arbor Low, Carl Wark (hill-fort), Castleton (Peveril Castle, caves), Chatsworth, Dovedale, Edale, Eyam, Flash, Goyt Valley, Haddon Hall, Hartington, Kinder Scout, Lathkill Dale, Lyme Hall and Country Park, Manifold Valley, Mam Tor, Miller's Dale (Chee Tor), Monsal Head, The Roaches, Robin Hood's Stride and Rowtor Rocks, Tideswell, Tissington, The Winnats, Winster

Parc Cenedlaethol Penfro
Pembrokeshire Coast

Around the edges of the main peninsula of West Wales lies the smallest in area of the ten national parks, the Pembrokeshire Coast. Alone of the ten it does not have an extensive tract of mountain or moorland as its main qualification, but a magnificent and varied coastline of 168 miles. One is never far from the sea in Pembrokeshire, for no part of the county is as much as ten miles from tidal water, and there are continual reminders of its presence in the climate, topography and history of the area. The 225 square miles of the park are divided into four areas, two of them almost entirely coastal, one including as well as coast a tract of high moorland known as the Presely (and sometimes called the Prescelly Hills), and the fourth an inland sector enclosing the wooded reaches of the Cleddau rivers. The park's designation was confirmed in 1952.

Much of South Pembrokeshire has a level appearance which belies the complexity of the rocks that lie beneath it, but even so the generally east-west grain of the country can be made out from the deep grooves of the river valleys and the low ridges between. Two sets of earth movements, over 200 and 300 million years ago, crunched the ancient rocks of Pembrokeshire up against the high land mass of Central Wales, forming the sharp folds that can be so clearly seen in some of the cliff sections. The fact that the grain of the country is end-on to the main attack of the waves, and that there are hard and soft rocks as well as lines of structural strength and weakness, is reflected in the variety of the cliff scenery, with broad bays, narrow inlets, rugged headlands, stacks and islands. In the Carboniferous Limestone between Tenby and Milford Haven, there are numerous blow-holes in the cliff edges, and a fine example of a natural arch—a stage in the formation of a stack—in the Green Bridge of Wales. Cliffs of Old Red Sandstone, volcanic rocks of the Ordovician age, Silurian limestones, Cambrian sandstones and conglomerates, and granites of Pre-Cambrian age, add to the colour and contrast of the coastline farther round and into North Pembrokeshire.

Dylan Thomas, at Laugharne, which lies a bit farther east on Carmarthen Bay, wrote of 'the see-saw sea' with more truth than he knew, for its level has not always been where it is now. About ten million years ago the sea was at work planing the rocks of the southern part of the county to a surface which is now at about 200 feet above sea level. In between, the sea level was much

'The Wash' on the limestone coast of South Pembrokeshire, near St Govan's Head.

lower than today's level, but at the close of the Ice Age it rose again to drown the river valleys, forming the deep-water anchorage of Milford Haven and the long creeks of the Cleddau rivers penetrating far inland. The surrounding sea, warmed by the Gulf Stream, provides Pembrokeshire with a mild, if moist, climate. Winters are almost frost-free, grass grows all the year round, and early potatoes are grown in the coastal areas. But the winds off the sea keep down tree growth, other than in the shelter of the narrow valleys and havens, and account for the rather bare appearance of much of the landscape.

Pwllderi and the rugged cliffs of North Pembrokeshire, near Strumble Head.

Rainfall ranges from 32 inches around the coast to as much as 80 inches on the Presely.

The good growing climate brings Spring early to Pembrokeshire, and colour to the cliffs and field banks. Sea pinks, stonecrop, wild thyme and gorse all make brilliant patterns of colour, but the magical blue of vernal squills is a special feature of the coast. Spring is also a better time than high summer for those interested in the seabirds of the park or in a trip to see the seal colonies on the islands. The largest breeding colony of grey seals in Wales is on Ramsey Island. Other island reserves are St Margaret's and Skokholm (West Wales Naturalists' Trust), Grassholm (like Ramsey, a Royal Society for the Protection of Birds reserve), and Skomer, a national nature reserve

Tenby's North Beach and the Goscar Rock.

owned by the Nature Conservancy and leased to the West Wales Naturalists' Trust. Trips to Skomer are included in the programme of the Pembrokeshire Countryside Unit (see p. 111).

Pembrokeshire is a county rich in antiquity, and its list of ancient monuments of all kinds is a formidable one. Old Stone Age remains have been
found in caves near Tenby and Pembroke, and Middle Stone Age implements and fragments occur in places on the coast in quantities that indicate
the presence of chipping floors and, probably, an export industry. The New
Stone Age has left some of the most impressive megalithic monuments in
Wales within the park boundaries. The best known of several fine burial
chambers, boulders set on end and often supporting capstones, is Pentre Ifan
on the northern edge of the Presely, with its 16-foot capstone on three tall
pillars. Others are Llech-y-Drybedd (Tripod Stone) between Newport and
Moylgrove, Carreg Samson near Trevine, and, of the three known examples
in the south of the county, the Devil's Quoit at the neck of the Angle
Peninsula. Just north of Mynachlog-ddu on the slopes of the Presely is the

104

Sandtop Bay and the tip of Caldey Island, looking towards St Margaret's Island and the mainland.

70-foot stone circle of Y Gors Fawr, but the Presely is more famous for its connection with a much more famous circle—Stonehenge. From Carn Menyn, also at the eastern end of the range, came the 'bluestones', some thirty of them, that were transported to Salisbury Plain.

The position of Pembrokeshire on a trade route to Ireland was important during the Bronze Age, and tracks marked by burial mounds can be followed over the Presely and also along the Ridgeway in the south of the county. Promontory and hill-top forts are the most striking reminders of Iron Age occupation; they served as defended platforms from which the inhabitants could farm the land near by. On St David's Head is a promontory fort or 'rath', and a series of earth and stone banks still used for today's field boundaries, perhaps a record for continuous farming use.

The names of Saint Ann, Saint Govan, Saint Ishmael, Saint Bride, Saint Non and Saint Dogmael are scattered over the map of Pembrokeshire, around the central focus of St David's. This was a point where the east-west route into and out of Ireland crossed the path of the Celtic missionaries

The moorland part of the park, looking eastwards along the Presely from Mynydd Bach

northwards through the Irish Sea. The cathedral of St David's, largely
twelfth century, stands on the site of an earlier monastic settlement founded
by the sixth-century St David, patron saint of Wales, and the Welsh name
of the city is Tŷdewi, the house of David. It is a remarkable site; the
cathedral, with its simple purplish sandstone exterior and its rich and oddly
sloped interior (it drops 14 feet from altar to West front), shelters in a hollow
by the River Alun, almost hidden from view, particularly towards the sea,
which in those early days brought as many raiders as pilgrims. The place-
names around the coast (Skokholm, Caldey, Gelliswick, Goodwick) are
evidence of the attentions of the Vikings during the sixth to ninth centuries,
and there is also evidence of settlement: a blood group common in West
Norway is found to occur significantly among some of the old-established
Pembrokeshire families.

The invisible line that divides the dominantly Welsh North Pembrokeshire from the more English South—often referred to as 'Little England beyond Wales'—also has a name of Norse origin, the 'Landsker'. Norman
influence was stronger in the south, and a line of castles traces the approximate

Pentre Ifan, one of the most spectacular of the burial chambers on and around the Presely.

boundary across the county from Roch, near Newgale, to Amroth on Car-marthen Bay. There are no fewer than fifteen stone-built castles, mostly of thirteenth-century construction, in Pembrokeshire, as well as some thirty-five motte, motte-and-bailey, and other earthwork fortifications of Norman date. Eight of the stone castles (Benton, Carew, Manorbier, Nevern, New-port, Picton, Tenby and Upton) lie within the park boundaries and, to-gether with the others, their construction and reconstruction provides a fascinating history of mediaeval fortification.

Wiston Castle, one of the chain on the Landsker, derives its name from Wizo, a twelfth-centry Flemish settler. The Flemings were industrious immi-grants who established prosperous agricultural and trading communities in the south during the reign of Henry I and after. Trading by sea remained an important part of Pembrokeshire life up to the nineteenth century and the coming of the railways. Coal and limestone from the south of the county were shipped around the coast and burnt for lime at many tiny havens where the old kiln remains can still be seen. From the larger ports like Haverfordwest trading vessels went to all parts of the world; many of the old warehouses can

107

St Govan's Chapel, a small (20 feet by 12 feet) stone building in a cleft of the cliffs near St Govan's Head.

be seen in the town, the inn by the old quay is called 'The Bristol Trader', and the Mayor has a second title of Admiral. Milford Haven was for long an important station of the Fleet, and now its natural deep-water anchorage has been deepened to provide the county with its new boom trade in oil. Tankers of up to 250,000 tons use the Haven, and the shores have sprouted colonies of storage tanks and other installations as well as an oil-fired power station with a 750-foot chimney.

The industrial expansion around Milford Haven is one of the problems which the park planning authority has had to face. At Popton and Gellis-

Manorbier Castle, birthplace of Giraldus Cambrensis, the twelfth-century Welsh chronicler.

wick installations spill over the park boundaries, but it has been possible by landscaping and sinking the bases of the storage tanks to reduce the impact of these onshore works. The tankers themselves are an impressive sight as they enter the Haven, and many visitors go to vantage points like St Ann's Head to watch them. Another of the park's problems has been the effect of the numerous war-time establishments, most now derelict, on the flat coastal landscape; some of these blemishes have been cleared away, but the scale of the problem really calls for national effort. Service training areas remain in the park, unfortunately including some of the best stretches of coastal scenery from Freshwater West to St Govan's Head, and around Manorbier.

A group of pony trekkers halts on the slopes of the Presely.

Some half a million people visit the Pembrokeshire Coast National Park and surrounding countryside every year. On the largely treeless coastal regions caravans can have a damaging effect on the beauty of the park, and the planning authority has sought to contain development within a few selected areas and to discontinue some of the more obtrusive sites. Besides the sandy beaches and the spectacular coastal scenery, the park offers a wide range of outdoor recreation opportunity: sailing and boating on the coast and on the reaches of the Cleddau rivers, walking and pony trekking on the Presely, sea and freshwater fishing. Except in the Tenby area, which is relatively accessible to the South Wales centres of population, most of the park is beyond the normal range of day visitors. Through the park runs the 168-mile Pembrokeshire Coast Path (see p. 219).

The Pembrokeshire National Park Committee is a separate committee of the County Council, which is planning authority for the park. Its offices are in Haverfordwest, where there is an information centre in the County Museum. Other information centres are at Tenby, Pembroke and St David's, and at Broad Haven there is the Pembrokeshire Countryside Unit set up by the Countryside Commission and the Field Studies Council in 1970. This has a purpose-built headquarters adjoining the car park, and from it an annual programme of conducted walks, tours and lectures is organized to help visitors to the park learn and understand more of the coast and countryside that lies around. To get the most out of a visit, it is advisable to find out the day's programme in advance and arrange to go on these outdoor excursions, but the Unit building also contains an information counter, has numerous books and leaflets and a small display area. Another popular feature is a daily weather forecast for the surrounding area, which is posted on a large board just outside the Unit.

CENTRES   Fishguard, Haverfordwest, Milford Haven, Pembroke, St Davids, Saundersfoot, Tenby

PLACES OF INTEREST   Amroth, Bosherston, Broad Haven (Pembrokeshire Countryside Unit), Caldey Island, Carew (Castle and cross), Carn Ingli, Carn Menyn, Carreg Samson, Dale, Lawrenny, Manorbier, Nevern, Newgale, Newport, Pentre Ifan, St Davids (Cathedral and Bishop's Palace), Solva, Tenby (Castle, walls, Tudor merchant's house)

Parc Cenedlaethol Eryri
Snowdonia National Park

Gwynedd, strongest and best defended of the ancient realms of the Welsh Princes, had a natural fortress in the mountains of North Wales. These mountains, the wooded valleys and the high, exposed passes that divide them, the moorlands that surround them and the tumbling streams that drain them are today part of a rather differently defended landscape—the Snowdonia National Park. The park was one of the three chosen by the National Parks Commission as their first year's target and was designated in 1952.

The name Snowdonia might suggest an area somewhat smaller than that selected for the park; it is sometimes applied to the mountains immediately surrounding Snowdon. But this is the second largest of the ten national parks. Its 845 square miles stretch from Penmaenmawr to the mouth of the Dovey, and include the Arennig, Aran and Rhinog ranges, and Cader Idris. On the west there are some twenty-three miles of coastline on Cardigan Bay, from Harlech to Aberdovey, and on the east the park boundary runs from Bala Lake (Llyn Tegid), the largest natural lake in Wales, across the marshy moorland of the Migneint to the valley of the River Conwy. From Nantlle through Llanberis to Aber the boundary is drawn to exclude some of the more extensive slate quarrying areas, as it is around the famous slate town of Blaenau Ffestiniog. In the south-east the park boundary mostly follows that of the county of Merioneth.

Although the park includes the highest land in England and Wales, culminating in the 3560 feet of Snowdon, it is a highly eroded land surface. The mountains are in fact no more than the worn-down stubs of the vast and ancient rock folds raised up in earth movements more than 300 million years ago. The rocks included huge thicknesses of volcanic ashes as well as the beds of shale which, under the conditions of great heat and pressure, became the slates of the area. When rock folds are worn down, the upfolds, or anticlines, are more easily eroded than the downfolds, or synclines, in which the rocks have been subject to more pressure. So it is that Snowdon itself is part of a syncline; the summit of volcanic rock is flanked on either side by inward-dipping rocks which help give the characteristic stepped appearance of the group. Southwards the Harlech dome has been worn away to expose much older rocks than those of Snowdon, and farther south still

IV.   Snowdonia National Park: a trout stream below Cnicht.

The view from the Porthmadog embankment, looking across the estuary towards Cnicht and the Moelwyns.

is the great north-facing cliff of Cader Idris, where the rocks are again dipping away towards the edge of the park area.

The last scouring of the land surface in this history of erosion was by the glaciers of the Ice Age, and the whole area is classic ground for the study of the effects of glaciation. There are fine examples of rock platforms scratched by the ice at Nant Peris, which like Nant Ffrancon, is a typical U-shape in cross-section. Steep sides and a flat valley floor indicate here, as in the Lake District, where glaciers carved and deepened the existing valleys. On the high ground the effects are just as noticeable. A glacier generally starts with an accumulation of snow and ice in a mountain hollow, and the movement downwards and outwards from the back of the hollow deepens it to a basin

The steep-sided valley of the Afon Glaslyn.

Castell y Gwynt (Castle of the Winds) on the left, and in the background Glyder Fawr (3279 ft).

shape. Standing on the summit of Snowdon one can easily see what results when several of these basins or *cwms* occur back to back; steep ridges are left separating them. On Cader Idris there is a particularly spectacular example of a *cwm*—the great semicircular hollow that holds Llyn Cau, so dramatically painted by Richard Wilson in the picture which now hangs in London's Tate Gallery.

Though there are a few north-flowing streams like those in the two valleys mentioned above, and the Conway, which forms the park boundary in the north-east, most of the streams and rivers follow a north-east to south-west pattern along the axis lines of the great folds. Often the rivers have found out the lines of weakness, as in the long valley running north-east to Bala and the Talyllyn valley running south-west to the coast. Along this line a great horizontal rock movement, or fault, shifted the mountain masses and produced a belt of broken material easily penetrated by the streams. The valley

Looking down Llyn Ogwen in winter towards the snow-covered slopes of Y Garn (left) and Foel Goch.

mouths, over-deepened by glaciation, make a trio of noble estuaries where the Dovey, Mawddach and Dwyryd reach Cardigan Bay.

There is a splendid range of vegetation in the park, from the sand dune and marshy areas on the coast to the mountain tops. With such variety of habitat a large proportion of British flowering plants are represented in the park. A link with Ice Age times is provided by the arctic-alpine plants which grow in several of the upland nature reserves, generally on rocky ledges and in north-facing *cwms*. Among them is the early-flowering Purple Saxifrage, often noticeable before the end of February. The survival of these plants after their favoured conditions had disappeared from most of England and Wales shows how little things have changed in the higher mountain regions. For though much of Snowdonia, like the rest of the country, was at one time clothed in forest, there was always some land left above the tree line. Then the trees too disappeared in all but a few places, under the influence of man, who is now, however, planting more than he is felling in the region. Clearance by settlers, by invaders, and the prevention of natural regeneration because of the grazing activities of sheep, accounted for the disappearance of much of the native ash and oak woods, but there are some splendid examples

Cwm Idwal nature reserve and the descent from Twll Du (The Devil's Kitchen); in the middle distance is Llyn Idwal and in the background Pen yr Olau Wen, the southern end of the Carnedd range.

remaining and now protected, as at Coed Camlyn and Coeddydd Maent-wrog in the Vale of Ffestiniog. These are two of the fifteen national nature reserves within the park; the others include Morfa Dyffryn and Morfa Har-lech on the coast, mountain areas on Cader Idris, the Rhinogs and Snowdon, and two notable *cwms*, Cwm Idwal and Cwm Glas Crafnant. Permits to visit are required for the coastal and woodland areas, though not for the open mountain areas.

The woodland parts of nature reserves have to be fenced against the depre-dations of livestock, which would quickly destroy young seedlings and under-growth. In most of Snowdonia livestock means sheep. It has been reckoned that for every person resident in the national park there are twenty-five sheep, a figure probably beaten only by Northumberland among the other parks. But

Llyn Llydaw and Snowdon.

The Mawddach estuary in winter, from near Barmouth.

An essentially Welsh scene of water, stone, whitewashed farm, hill pasture, woodland and mountain. The bridge is on Afon Dysynni, not far from Castell y Bere.

there are cattle too, often the characteristic Welsh Blacks, wherever there is sufficient valley floor land to give them pasture as well as providing for hay and other winter feeding crops. The in-by land, which lies below the mountain sheepwalk and is separated from it by the 'ffridd' wall, consists of a number of fields which represent the sheep-farmer's filing system for his sheep. They must be carefully split up and segregated at particular times of year to keep rams from ewes, or ewes from lambs. The importance of the stone walls, so often damaged carelessly by those who fail to appreciate the nimbleness or opportunism of the sheep, cannot be over-emphasised.*

While hill-farming is the most immediately noticeable industry in the park, forestry, quarrying, electricity generation and light industry also play their part in the park's economy. The Forestry Commission have four forests in the area—Gwydyr, Coed y Brenin, Beddgelert and Aberhirnant—and part of the Dovey Forest in the south lies within the park boundaries. Gwydyr is the nucleus of the Commission's Forest Park, with a car park and Arboretum on the A5 road some three miles west of Betws y Coed, picnic sites, forest trails and many waymarked walks. The slate industry having declined, quarrying and mining is no longer so active, and there are many abandoned sites, some of which are being considered for their industrial archaeological value. Opinions may differ about the contribution made to the interest of the park by Trawsfynydd nuclear power station or the Tanygrisiau pumped storage scheme above the Vale of Ffestiniog, but there is no doubt that many people take advantage of the arrangements made for parties to visit these industrial monuments. Three woollen mills in the park, at Bryncir near Porthmadog, at Trefriw and near Dinas Mawddwy, are all open to visitors and have attractive finished products on sale.

Snowdonia's mountains are the highest in England and Wales with many of the finest rock climbs and first-class hill walking. The Centre run by the Central Council of Physical Recreation at Plas y Brenin, near Capel Curig, has been the training ground of many famous expeditions to the highest mountain ranges in the world. In fact, Snowdonia can provide testing conditions for the toughest and most experienced mountaineer, which makes all the more alarming the unpreparedness of some who venture on to the mountains. Every Easter brings worry to the mountain rescue teams from those who refuse to believe that we have any mountains worth the name and gaily set off without the proper clothing, training or experience.

Snowdon, 'that monstrous height' as Defoe described it, was acquired by the nation in 1968 with some 13,000 acres which were formerly part of the Vaynol Estate. The summit will be kept in public ownership together with any bottom land required for car parks, picnic and camping sites, while the

* Farm 'trails' setting out the story of the upland sheep farm have been established at Gwern Gof Uchaf in the Ogwen Valley and near Llanbedr on the slopes of the Rhinog range.

Climbing instruction at Capel Curig.

remainder will be disposed of subject to arrangements for public access. For Snowdon is inexhaustibly popular, a thousand people a day making for its summit during holiday times. There are several routes of different lengths up Snowdon, but erosion from climbers' boots has badly affected some, and extra care now has to be taken on the two eastern ascents and the Watkin Path in their steepest parts.

The easy way up Snowdon is, of course, by the mountain railway, which must have carried millions there since 1896, when it started. It is the only rack railway in the British Isles. Two other narrow-gauge railways in the park also attract a lot of attention: the Festiniog runs from Porthmadog up the northern side of the Vale of Ffestiniog and will eventually be extended beyond its present mountain terminus of Dduallt; the Talyllyn runs from Tywyn to Abergynolwyn.

Not far from the inland terminus of the Talyllyn Railway is Castell y Bere, the ruins of an old Welsh fortress. Its impressive site may be compared with two other Welsh castles, Dolbadarn, guarding the Llanberis Pass, and Dolwyddelan, once the home of Llywelyn the Great. But the most visited castle in the park is the Norman and mediaeval Harlech, with its complicated fortifications and history. The earlier antiquities too should not be forgotten, for, as Defoe pointed out, with pardonable exaggeration, 'whoever travels critically over these mountains . . . will think Stonehenge in Wiltshire and Roll-Rich Stones in Oxfordshire no more a wonder'. The stone circle on Penmaenmawr Mountain (partly for the view) and the elaborate burial chamber at Capel Garmon help bear out this judgment though, and there are certainly numerous hut circles, standing stones, cairns and camps to track down on the hillsides. Romans, while probably unconnected with the Roman Steps at Cwm Bychan, have also left remains of several camps and forts at strategic valley sites.

For the motorist Snowdonia is a park with a number of fine passes to top, one of the highest being the Bwlch y Groes between Dinas Mawddwy and Llanuwchllyn at 1790 feet. This and several of the other high passes are traversed by mountain roads (single track) on which it is important to remember that the passing places are not parking places. A number of circuits have been worked out by the park authorities, who have also put in car parks at strategic points, such as that at the summit of the Crimea Pass; details of these circuits can be obtained from the park information offices.

Snowdonia National Park lies mostly in the counties of Merioneth and Caernarvon, with a small part in Denbighshire. There are three separate park committees and a Joint Advisory Committee. A planning consultant and an information officer are employed jointly for the park. Information centres have been set up at Bala, Blaenau Ffestiniog, Dolgellau, Harlech, Llanrwst and Llanberis, and a purpose-built centre has just been opened at Aberdovey.

At Plas Tanybwlch, near Maentwrog, a residential study centre is being planned. Holiday chalets have been erected by the Denbighshire Committee on a site at Llanrwst on the park boundary and these 'Hafotai' provide good self-catering accommodation.

Two physical features of Snowdonia—its old, mineralized rocks, and its high mountain valleys—have recently made the park attractive to teams looking for gold and copper and for a new pumped storage scheme site. Despite objections that exploitation of any findings of gold in the Mawddach Estuary or copper in the Coed y Brenin area would be quite unacceptable in the national park, explorations at both sites have been carried out. The subject of the pumped storage investigations was Llyn Peris, in a popular valley though also an area scarred by the enormous Dinorwic slate quarries.

CENTRES   Bala, Bangor, Barmouth, Betws y Coed, Caernarvon, Capel Curig, Conway, Harlech, Llandudno, Llanrwst, Machynlleth

PLACES OF INTEREST   Aber Falls, Aberglaslyn Pass, Abergynolwyn, Beddgelert, Brithdir (Torrent Walk), Bryncir (woollen mill), Capel Garmon (cromlech), Castell y Bere, Conwy Falls, Cwm Idwal, Cymmer Abbey, Dolwyddelan Castle, Gwydyr Castle, Harlech Castle, Llyn Padarn country park, Maentwrog, Meirion Mill (Dinas Mawddwy), North Wales Quarrying Museum (Dinorwic), Penmaenmawr, Precipice Walk (Nannau), Railways (Snowdon Mountain, Festiniog, Talyllyn), Roman Steps (Cwm Bychan), Tomen y Mur (fort), Trefriw (woollen mill), Tremadoc

Yorkshire Dales

Yorkshire boasts two of the ten national parks of England and Wales and shares in a third. The Yorkshire Dales National Park lies in the north-west of the county, half in the North Riding and half in the West Riding, firmly astride the great watershed of the Pennines. It is a large park, and its 680 square miles is exceeded only by the Lake District and Snowdonia parks. Stone and water are the two principal elements of the landscape: limestone scars fringe the broad dales, stone bridges span the streams and rivers, grey stone farms and villages blend with their surroundings, and underground watercourses penetrate miles under the moorland. The southern parts of the park have for long been popular with walkers, climbers and cavers from the industrial West Riding; the northern parts offer more wild, remote areas with fewer settlements. The national park was the seventh to be designated, in 1954.

From Skipton the south-west boundary of the park follows roughly the line of the A65 road to Kendal as far as the county boundary just beyond Ingleton. Here the park boundary follows that of the county northwards by Sedbergh and along the edge of the Lune gorge, overlooking the new M6 motorway, to Uldale Head in the Howgill Fells, and on eastwards across the Mallerstang to Tan Hill. Rounding the head of Arkengarthdale, the park boundary follows the high ground down to Swaledale and extends in a long arm along the river almost as far as Richmond, doubling back and curving south-west to Castle Bolton on the edge of Wensleydale. It then crosses the mouth of Coverdale, and, at East Witton, turns south-west again to the summit of Great Whernside, before continuing south to the Wharfe at Bolton Abbey. This vast area encloses the east-flowing rivers of Swale and Ure, the western dales of Dent and Garsdale, and the south-flowing Ribble, Aire and Wharfe dales, together with their tributaries.

The bulk of the park consists of a wide platform of Carboniferous rocks—limestone in the south dipping gently northwards and eastwards to disappear under more mixed beds of shale, sandstone and limestones and eventually under the Millstone Grit. Remnants of the Millstone Grit covering cap the higher hills to give them their characteristic stepped profiles. Another immediately noticeable feature is the Craven Fault system which, near Settle, almost coincides with the park boundary. The rocks to the south have slipped downwards as much as 5000 feet, so that the Millstone Grit lies alongside the

Gordale Scar, a steep gorge cut into the Great Scar Limestone of the southern part of the park.

lower limestones, and this displacement shows in the cliffs of Giggleswick Scar, Attermire Scar and, farther east, in Malham Cove and Gordale Scar. In the west another great fracture, the Dent Fault, has thrown the limestone against the older rocks of the Howgill Fells. The oldest rocks of all occur in the Ingleton and Austwick areas, where slates and grits of Pre-Cambrian age can be seen in the rocky courses of the streams. The small inliers of such places as Crummackdale are a classical field study ground for first-year students of geology.

The effect of the Ice Age on the scenery is also easily to be seen in the park, in the shapes of the main dales with their wide floors, mounds of clay and

Limestone scenery of the Craven country: Malham Cove, abandoned as a waterfall when the water found a way out under the foot of the cliffs.

rock debris, and the two natural areas of water—Malham Tarn and Semerwater—which rest in hollows scooped out and dammed by the ice. An impressive demonstration of the force of this ice can be seen just east of Clapham, where the Norber boulders, massive chunks of dark slate, have been left perched incongruously on the white limestone pavement. In the museums at Skipton and Settle can be seen remains of animals from the warmer postglacial period which were found in the caves of the area, also evidence of later human occupation of the caves.

On the undisturbed hillsides may be seen the marks of Bronze and Iron Age settlers in the area: barrows, hut circles, earthworks and ancient field systems. The Romans had a lead-mining interest in the east of the park area and maintained a military presence with roads over the moors linking small forts. The site of one such fort can be seen at Bainbridge, standing on high ground just east of the village.

Trees growing from the limestone pavement above Chapel le Dale. In the background is the characteristic profile of Ingleborough, one of the famous 'Three Peaks'.

Lead mining, followed by coal mining for domestic heating and for lime burning, continued to be important activities for many centuries, and the pits, chimneys and workings have left a rich industrial archaeology interest in the park. Today the major industry is the quarrying of limestone, particularly in Wharfedale and Ribblesdale, and the heavy lorry traffic on some of the narrow village roads is something of a problem. The earlier mining industries, with their smaller-scale activity, had rather different transport problems and solved them by the network of tracks and green roads over the moors which today provides such fine routes for walkers.

Farming is, however, the main occupation of the dalesman, and in this country, with a heavy rainfall and only a small proportion of flat valley land, this means either sheep or cattle. Most dales farms keep both, using their richer valley land for cattle and for hay and putting their sheep on rough and fell grazing for most of the year. Though most milk now goes out of the area, some Wensleydale Cheese is still made at Hawes. Sheep, of course, go out

'Stone and water are the two principal elements of the landscape'; Buckden Beck at the head of Wharfedale.

of the area too, and not just for winter fattening in the lowlands; Dales stock is justly famous and the Swaledale breeds are widespread elsewhere.

The moorland which is grazed by the sheep varies in its covering from the thin vegetation of the southern limestone areas to the tussocky peat areas of the high land in the central and northern parts of the park. Heather moor is found chiefly on the grit lands in the east and north, and with it the red

The broader, more pastoral Wensleydale, showing the typical stone walls and farm outbuildings.

grouse. One of the most attractive stretches is the grouse moor at Barden, where the park authority has a public access agreement with the estate of the Duke of Devonshire. The two national nature reserves in the park are small

The famous multiple falls at Aysgarth in Wensleydale, where the park authority has provided extra car parking, an information centre and waymarked walks.

but valuable historic remnants. At Ling Gill, high up in Ribblesdale, a steep wooded ravine has preserved some of the tree species which were once common over the limestone areas, and a little to the south-east at Colt Park

The village of Bainbridge, since Roman times an important crossing for the old routes over the fells.

Wood (permit required) ash and other trees can be seen growing from the fissures of the bare rock.

The limestone pavements of the Craven area are one of the park's most distinctive features, and can be seen at their best just above Malham Cove. In the same way that the joints of the pavements are enlarged by solution, the great cave and pothole systems of the park began to extend underground.

The older rocks of the Howgill Fells, in the north-west corner of the park, give a distinctive rounded profile.

The exploring of their strange and often beautiful world is a matter for the experienced and well equipped party, but there are caves on view at White Scar just north of Ingleton, on Ingleborough not far from Clapham, and over to the east at Stump Cross.

While most of the climbing is done underground in this park, there are many short climbs on limestone and gritstone outcrops. But walking is the main recreation, and there are many splendid routes from dale to dale, some of them following the old drovers' routes, like Mastiles Lane, from Wharfe-dale to Malhamdale, or the old roads from Bainbridge and Hawes in Wensleydale over into Ribblesdale. The last of these coincides with the line of the Pennine Way (see p. 223), which threads its way through the park from Gargrave in the south to the isolated Tan Hill in the north. The Three Peaks of Ingleborough (2373 feet), Whernside (2419 feet) and Pen-y-Ghent (2273 feet) provide a tough fitness test when tackled together in the famous circuit, but are all worthwhile ascents with good views. There are also good

Traditionally Dales life is that of a tightly knit community; this is Arkengarthdale, once prominent for lead-mining.

roads up the main dales and some testing mountain roads; the park information service has published a scenic drive route encompassing the best of the Craven country for nearly fifty miles between Clapham and Skipton.

Each of the dales has its individual character and attractions, and most regular visitors to the park will have their favourites. Wharfedale is one of the longest and full of enchanting villages—Buckden, Kettlewell, Linton, Burnsall and Appletreewick. The little town of Grassington makes a good centre. The dale also includes, just within the park, the fourteenth-century ruins of Bolton Priory and its grounds, in which the Wharfe squeezes itself through the narrow chasm known as the Strid. In Airedale there are the great limestone features of Malham Cove and Gordale Scar at the head of the dale; in Ribblesdale the dominating profiles of Ingleborough and Pen-y-Ghent; in Wensleydale the triple waterfall of Aysgarth, the village of Bainbridge, more fine waterfalls like Hardraw and Mossdale at the valley edges, and the great castle of Bolton, once the prison of Mary, Queen of Scots. In the north,

Swaledale can be reached by the famous Buttertubs Pass from Wensleydale, and near Keld there is another fine group of falls. The two north-west dales of Dent and Garsdale are shorter and more secluded. Dent Town retains its old cobbled streets and has one of the highest railway stations in the country, over four miles away and some 1200 feet above sea level. Cautley Spout, in the Rawthey Valley off Garsdale and not far from the main town of Sedbergh, has a fall of over 800 feet. The tributary dales of Littondale and Langstrothdale (Wharfedale); Bishopdale, Coverdale and Widdale (Wensleydale); and Arkengarthdale and Birkdale (Swaledale), are all worth several days' exploration.

The Yorkshire Dales is as yet a park free from overcrowding, except at one or two places. Both Malham in the West Riding and Aysgarth in the North get considerable numbers of visitors at holiday times, and the park authorities have here put in car parks and information points to cope with the pressure. But in the park as a whole there is plenty of space. Building control is important in an area where the character of the towns and villages and of the countryside generally is so dependent on the use of local materials, and the West Riding Council has published a guide on the subject.

One matter which has raised a great deal of argument is afforestation: there is not yet much forest in the park, and a proposal for plantings in Langstrothdale brought many protests from amenity interests. There will undoubtedly be pressure for forestry licences in some of the dales, but a good deal of the land in the park is unsuitable for afforestation not only for amenity reasons but because trees are unlikely to grow successfully.

The national park is administered by the North and West Riding County Councils, who are the planning authorities for the two halves of the park, and there is a Joint Advisory Committee of the two. Information centres have been established at Aysgarth, Clapham and Malham, and the joint information service operates from Harrogate.

CENTRES   Grassington, Harrogate, Ilkley, Richmond, Sedbergh, Settle, Skipton

PLACES OF INTEREST   Airton, Appletreewick, Askrigg, Aysgarth, Bainbridge, Bolton Abbey, Buckden, Burnsall, Buttertubs Pass, Castle Bolton, Cautley Spout, Clapham, Coverham Abbey, Dent Town, Giggleswick Scar, God's Bridge (Ingleton Glen), Gordale Scar, Hardraw Force, Ingleborough, Kilnsey Crag, Malham Cove and Tarn, Pen-y-Ghent, Semerwater, The Strid, Stump Cross Cavern, Tan Hill, Thornton Force, Whernside

2
AREAS OF OUTSTANDING
NATURAL BEAUTY

The thirty-one designated areas of outstanding natural beauty which are described in the following pages are representative of almost every kind of landscape to be found in England and Wales. They vary greatly in size; the largest, North Wessex Downs, is exceeded in area by only three of the national parks, while the smallest extends to only twenty-two square miles, in Dedham Vale. No special arrangements are required for their planning, as with national parks, though some of the areas have appointed advisory committees or standing conferences with memberships which include local amenity or natural history interests.

The designation of these areas arises from a joint decision by local authorities and the Countryside Commission on a boundary within which the coast or countryside has character and quality that is worthy of special attention in planning and development control. The Commission makes the designation, submitting the map of the area to the Secretary of State for the Environment or the Secretary of State for Wales to be confirmed. The original programme of areas considered by the Commission for designation in this way stems from the 'conservation areas' of the Hobhouse Report of 1947. But many county councils have pressed for designation of particular areas to strengthen their hand in controlling development. The process of designation continues; the greater part of the Lincolnshire Wolds was confirmed in April 1973 as the thirty-second area of outstanding natural beauty.

Anglesey

Anglesey, or English Island, first got this name in the times of Edward I, when the island was brought under English control and the fine castle of Beaumaris built. Indeed, Edward badly wanted a stone bridge across the Menai Straits to tie the island to the mainland, but was advised by his engineers that this was impossible; it took the genius of Telford, in 1826, to span the Straits, pioneering the suspension bridge method. The Welsh name of the island is Môn, and it has long been celebrated as the grand nursery of the Druids' religion.

Some eighty-four square miles of Anglesey were designated in 1966 as an area of outstanding natural beauty, the designation being confirmed the next year. The area consists of all but a few miles of the coast of the island and includes most of Holy Island also. Gaps at Amlwch, Benllech, Menai Bridge, Rhosneigr and Wylfa, cut out the relatively few developed areas of this fine coastline, with its rugged cliffs, small coves, sandy bays and warrens.

Some of the oldest rocks in Wales, squeezed into a series of folds from north-west to south-east, make up the foundation of Anglesey, and account for the low ridges and shallow valleys that run parallel to the Menai Straits. The latter is itself a valley or pair of valleys drowned during the period just after the Ice Age. The low plateau of the island, with its few isolated hills, contrasts sharply with the mountainous area of Snowdonia on the mainland, and is the result of the planing action of the sea at an earlier time, when most of Anglesey was below sea level, together with the low coastal strip on the mainland, and the coastline was right back against the mountains. Since the level of the land has risen again, the sea has fretted out the crescent-shaped bays and rocky headlands which make its present coastline so attractive.

The main road around the island affords access to most parts of the designated area, without spoiling the isolation of the coastline. From the Menai Bridge on the right hand lies Beaumaris, with its castle, famous old inns, and interesting seventeenth-century courthouse. Now a popular sailing centre with a regatta fortnight in August, it was once the principal town on the island. Beyond lies Penmôn, in Welsh the tip or head of the island, where there are the ruins of a priory and of a curious fifteenth-century dovecote, and, offshore, Priestholm or Puffin Island. Anglesey is one of the strongholds of the puffin or sea parrot, now protected, but which, according to earlier writers, 'being pickled forms a very delicate dish'. Northwards lie the small

Ynys Llandwyn (Newborough Warren), with the mountains of Snowdonia seen in the distance across the dunes of the national nature reserve.

and larger ports of Red Wharf Bay and Moelfre, and a wide bay popular with campers.

In the other direction from Menai Bridge one passes the lofty monument to the Marquess of Anglesey, of Waterloo fame, before coming to New-borough Warren, a national nature reserve rated very highly, with a wide range of habitats from rocky shores to dune systems. Aberffraw, farther round the coast, was, in the thirteenth century, the headquarters of Llywelyn the Great, to whom there is a modern memorial. The causeway to Holy Island leads to a more rugged landscape than that of the main island. Holy-head Mountain rises to 720 feet, with the Isle of Man and the hills of Co. Wicklow in Ireland visible from its summit. All Anglesey is a treasure-house of prehistoric remains, and two to be seen here are the old fort of Caer y Twr and the Cytiau'r Gwyddelod, or Irish huts. On the north coast of the main island are two fine areas of National Trust land at Cemaes Bay and Cemlyn Bay, the latter an Enterprise Neptune purchase. Between them lies Wylfa, excepted from the area on account of the nuclear power station there.

CENTRES Amlwch, Bangor, Beaumaris, Benllech, Holy-head, Llanfair P.G., Menai Bridge

PLACES OF INTEREST Holyhead Mountain, Beaumaris Castle, New-borough Warren, Penmon Priory, Moelfre, Aberffraw

Arnside and Silverdale

The most recently designated area of outstanding natural beauty, and one of the smallest, contains the villages of Arnside and Silverdale on the north-eastern shoreline of Morecambe Bay. Bounded on the north by the Kent estuary across which lies part of the Lake District National Park, and on the east by the A6 road between Carnforth and Milnthorpe, the area has as its western margin the wide expanse of sands stretching out towards the Kent Channel. The railway from the main line at Carnforth to Arnside and across the Kent viaduct to Grange-over-Sands threads its way through the area.

The mountain limestone of the southern fringes of the Lake District makes up the main features of this intimate and small-scale landscape. Arnside Knott, though only 500 feet high, gives splendid views over the ever-changing sands and tidal flats of the Bay to the Coniston and Central Fells of the Lake District. Piercing these limestone hills and knolls are stretches of woodland and low-lying areas known as 'mosses'. On the road from Carnforth to Silverdale lies the best-known of these mosses, Leighton Moss, a national wildfowl refuge managed by the Royal Society for the Protection of Birds.

The designated area, partly in Westmorland and partly in Lancashire, started with a less secure future than most. A proposal for the badly needed link road from the M6 motorway to far-off Barrow-in-Furness, which would have virtually bisected the area, was rejected, and indeed a road to industrial traffic standards would be totally out of keeping with the scale of this country-side. Then the long-discussed Morecambe Bay Barrage, which could itself provide a much better route for a Barrow link road to follow, would affect the shifting channels and sands which give such interest to this estuarial area. Two of the alternative schemes proposed in 1972 involve large fresh-water reservoirs out in the Bay and on Warton Sands.

Silverdale from near Jenny Brown's Point; in the background is Arnside Knot (right) and the sands of Morecambe Bay.

Cannock Chase

Cannock Chase, the second smallest designated area, was included in the National Parks Commission's programme at once, following visits by members of the Commission. They considered that its coal and gravel resources and the pressures of a population of $2\frac{1}{2}$ million within twenty miles made it especially vulnerable. It is an area of twenty-six square miles of high bracken-clad heathland and woodland with numerous attractive valleys, framed by low-lying country in which there are fine parklands and pleasant villages. Extending from Brocton to Rugeley and from Tixall to Gentleshaw, it also includes Shoal Hill Common to the south-west, just by Cannock.

The Chase encloses the last remnant of the old Cannock Forest which once stretched east to Tamworth and west to Wolverhampton. Much of the forest was oak, felled in great quantities during the sixteenth and seventeenth

Most of the old Cannock Forest has disappeared, and there is afforestation with pine among the areas of heath and bracken.

centuries for charcoal burning. Stripped of its cover, the higher part of the Chase became poorer and less fertile as the soil reverted to the thin, acid variety which is at first all that can be derived from the dry Bunter Sandstones of the North Midlands. Birch and pine are now commoner than oak on the Chase, but at Brocton Coppice the one remaining part of the old forest can be seen.

The area is rich in wild life, and there are several Sites of Special Scientific Interest scheduled by the Nature Conservancy. Staffordshire County Council established their first outdoor trail in the area in 1969, and in 1970 it won a European Conservation Year award. The trail, which follows the Sherbrook Valley, now links with two more—a short trail of fifteen to twenty minutes' walk from Seven Springs, and the Haywood Warren Trail which is about three miles across some of the wilder parts of the Chase. Fox, deer and badger are among the animals whose tracks cross the trails; the deer are Fallow, descendants of those which were once hunted on the Chase.

In the north of the area lies Shugborough, seat of the Earls of Lichfield, now owned by the National Trust and managed by the County Council. The house has extensive alterations and additions by Samuel Wyatt, and in the park is a group of remarkable monuments by James Stuart based on the Antiquities of Athens. Part of the house now contains the County Museum.

There is public access over more than 3000 acres of the wilder areas of the Chase, including 2100 acres at Brocton Field given to the County Council by the Earl of Lichfield in 1957. Part of this has been made a 'motorless zone', reserved entirely for walking, riding and similar activities. Much of the rest of the Chase is farmed or afforested; the Foresty Commission has over 6000 acres, mostly of Scots and Corsican Pine.

CENTRES   Cannock, Stafford, Rugeley, Lichfield

PLACES OF INTEREST   Shugborough Hall and Park, Castle Ring at Cannock Wood, outdoor trails at Seven Springs, Haywood Warren and Sherbrook Valley

Chichester Harbour

Chichester Harbour, with Langstone Harbour, is a low-lying area of the Hampshire Basin penetrated by the sea. The twenty-nine square mile area designated in 1963 (confirmed 1964) is bounded in the north by the A27 road from Havant to Chichester and in the south by the Harbour mouth. Extending from Hayling Island in the west to Apuldram in the east, it includes the whole of Thorney Island and the four main channels of the Harbour (Chichester, Bosham, Thorney and Emsworth). The county boundary between Hampshire and West Sussex runs up the centre of the Emsworth Channel, so that most of the designated area lies in Sussex.

One of the few remaining undeveloped coastal areas in southern England, Chichester Harbour remains, in parts, in a relatively wild state. Though there are rough grazings on land reclaimed from salt marsh and in the northern part of the area agricultural land of high value, within the Harbour are vast mats of Spartina or rice grass inundated at high tide. These and the stretches of sheltered water are a great attraction to wildfowl, and large numbers of Brent Geese winter in the area. In two woods on the shores of the Harbour are heronries.

In past centuries the Harbour was important for commerce. The Roman harbour site has still to be excavated, but on the edge of the area lies the famous Roman Palace of Fishbourne, part of which has been successfully uncovered and displayed. Corn and, later, wool were exported from the Harbour, but the east side gradually silted up and Emsworth grew as a port in consequence during the eighteenth century, as can be seen from its wealth of elegant Georgian buildings. All the ports dry out today so there is no commerce, and the bar across the mouth of the Harbour prevents the larger pleasure craft from getting in or out. But the area is one of the most popular sailing centres on the south coast. Chichester and Emsworth yacht basins and Birdham Pool have over a thousand berths between them.

Bosham is one of the popular villages with yachtsmen, and has a long history as a point of embarkation. 'Harold Dux Anglorum et sui milites equitant ad Bosham' the Bayeux Tapestry records, and, showing Harold wading to his ship with horse and hound, 'hic Harold mare navigavit'. There is a charming representation on the Tapestry of the church at Bosham where they prayed before setting out. Nowadays Harold might have had a job to find his way to clear water through the crowded moorings, for here, as at most places in the Harbour, demand exceeds the capacity. The control of the

143

Boats at Bosham quay; the Harbour is one of the most popular sailing centres on the South Coast.

western shore of the Thorney Channel by the Ministry of Defence, with consequent restriction of access, is one of the problems in planning the future of the Harbour. A national report on the planning of the coastline which was issued by the Countryside Commission in 1970 recommended Chichester Harbour as one of the first Regional Coastal Parks, and in 1971 the Chichester Harbour Conservancy Act provided for a unified authority to control and manage Chichester and Emsworth Harbours, together with a surrounding amenity area.

CENTRES   Chichester, Emsworth, Havant, Hayling Island

PLACES OF INTEREST   Bosham, Fishbourne Roman Palace, Langstone Harbour

144

Chilterns

One of the finest stretches of countryside within easy reach of London, the Chilterns lie to the north-west of the capital, a broad belt of woodland and downland seamed by dry valleys and peopled with flint-and-brick villages. The best of this countryside was included in the 309 square mile area of outstanding natural beauty designated in 1964. The area extends for nearly fifty miles from the Goring Gap, where the Thames cuts through the line of the chalk hills, north-eastwards almost to Hitchin; it varies from three to fourteen miles in width, and excludes the built-up High Wycombe, Chesham and Berkhamsted valleys and the Luton gap through which pass the motorway and mainline from London. The designation was confirmed in 1965.

The Chilterns are chalk hills, and the chalk here is dipping gently to the south-east where it passes beneath the clays and gravels of the London Basin. The steepest scarp slopes are produced from gently dipping or horizontal strata, and the Chilterns escarpment is the most prominent feature of the area. Overlooking the broad clay Vale of Aylesbury it rises to over 800 feet in places and provides some magnificent viewpoints. Deep coombes break up the line of the scarp, which is often well-wooded; the fine beeches that hide the diagonal line of Telford's road (A40) down Aston Hill are familiar to all travellers between London and Oxford. Although the typical chalk landscape of smooth, rounded hills, dry valleys and close, light-coloured turf, is to be seen within the area, particularly in the north-east part, much of the Chilterns has a cover of clay-with-flints, and flint gravels, derived from the steady erosion of the chalk over thousands of years. It is this cover that has supported the high proportion of woodland in the area; nearly one-fifth of the land carries trees, with beech the commonest.

Beech was a well-known resource of the area in the eighteenth century. 'The quantity of this brought from hence', wrote Defoe, 'is almost incredible,

Wood anemones in Chiltern beechwoods near Chesham, Buckinghamshire.

and yet so is the country overgrown . . . that it is bought very reasonable, nor is there like to be any scarcity of it for time to come.' At that time coppice beech was used as fuel, but, as coal became cheaper, the chief user became the furniture industry, which still thrives in High Wycombe. Bodgers, or woodland lathe-turners, fashioned legs and spindles for the characteristic Windsor-style chairs and other furniture on the spot, till mechanization of the industry eventually led to their disappearance; and changes in felling policy over the years have led to the decline of the beechwoods in this century. But there are still 33,000 acres of them.

A positive management policy for the Chilterns beechwoods is one of the valuable recommendations of the 'Plan for the Chilterns' published in 1971 by the Standing Conference which advises on the planning of the area. This body, representing the four county councils of the area—Bedfordshire, Buckinghamshire, Hertfordshire and Oxfordshire—together with the Countryside Commission, the Forestry Commission, Nature Conservancy and National Trust, has secured an encouragingly wide measure of agreement for the plan's conclusions.

The Chilterns Plan also includes proposals for coping with the pressures on the area for recreation. It is estimated that one-fifth of the population of England live within easy motoring distance, and the westward continuation of the M40, which crosses the area, will make communications even easier. Walking and riding are popular activities, for there is a good network of public footpaths and bridleways, but there are also many attractions that can be reached by car, including viewpoints on the scarp edge, stately homes, picturesque villages and parkland. The National Trust owns some well-known properties at Ashridge, Hughenden Manor and West Wycombe Park. An even better known (though private) property is Chequers, the Prime Minister's country home.

CENTRES	Amersham, Berkhamsted, Chesham, Dunstable, Henley, High Wycombe, Marlow, Princes Risborough, Tring, Wallingford
PLACES OF INTEREST	Aldbury, Ashridge Park, Barton Hills, Chenies, Christmas Common, Ewelme, Fingest, Goring, Greys Court (near Henley), Hughenden Manor, Ivinghoe Beacon, Little Gaddesden Manor, Mapledurham House, Stonor Park (near Henley), West Wycombe Park, Village, and Hell Fire Caves, Whipsnade Zoo

146

Cornwall

There are few parts of this country as fiercely individual as Cornwall. The River Tamar which separates it from England was for centuries the eastern boundary of a Celtic people with their own ways and language, though by the eighteenth century it could be recorded that Cornish had become nearly extinct 'owing to an increase of civilisation'. But civilisation is a relative matter and Cornwall had a head start: it was the landfall for the earliest Mediterranean traders and, through its copper and tin, was a centre of Bronze Age technology. It is indeed its history, as well as its coastal scenery and its climate, that makes Cornwall so attractive to holiday visitors and present-day settlers; the magic of Lyonesse still works.

The coast of Cornwall was among the ten national parks originally suggested by John Dower in 1945, and, though omitted from the lists of the Hobhouse Report two years later, was again considered for park status by the National Parks Commission in 1952. In 1955, however, the Commission decided that the 'long, narrow and discontinuous coastal stretches' which had been suggested would be more appropriate as an area of outstanding natural beauty, and the designation was completed in 1959.

The 360 square miles that were designated contain some of the finest coastal scenery in Britain, including many famous landmarks known internationally to seamen as well as to holidaymakers. There is a large part of the Land's End peninsula, a coastal strip from St Michael's Mount to Porthleven, the whole of the Lizard Peninsula, including the beautiful Helford Estuary, right up to the outskirts of Falmouth. The three other stretches of the south Cornwall coast are from St Mawes to St Austell, from Gribbin Head and the Fowey Estuary to West Looe, and from Rame Head to Mount Edgcumbe, overlooking Plymouth Sound. In North Cornwall the whole coastline between the boundary with Devon at Marsland Mouth and Bedruthan Steps, just north of Newquay, is included except for an area around Bude and part of the Camel Estuary between Polzeath and Padstow. Two further areas on the north coast are from Perranporth to Porthtowan and between Portreath and Godreavy Towans. Inland the granite mass of Bodmin Moor also forms part of the area.

Brown Willy and Rough Tor, the highest points of Bodmin Moor, afford a good general view of the level nature of the Cornish peninsula, which has been planed by the sea in past ages when it stood at very different levels from today's. The hilly areas that can be made out are the other resistant granite

'The granite mass of Bodmin Moor': the view from Catshole Tor.

masses, just north of St Austell, the moorland of Carnmenellis and Carn
Brea, and Land's End itself. These poke up through the surrounding slates,
sandstones and shales, and must at one time have formed islands, much as the
Scilly Isles do today. For although the ice of the Ice Age never reached this
part of England, its effects were felt in the risen sea level and in a tilting of the
peninsula from north to south as the weight of the ice mass left the lands to the

north. Now that the sea level is rising slowly again, the lower valleys of the rivers draining into the Channel have been drowned to form the beautiful inland havens of South Cornwall. The sea is again carving its way around the granite masses (as at Mounts Bay and St Ives Bay) to make an island out of the peninsula. The rocks of the Lizard call for special mention: they result from a much earlier and different kind of volcanic activity and have subse-quently been changed into the green, purple and mottled serpentines that give the cliffs their dramatic colouring.

Inland Cornwall is often dreary, with scars of mining, clay tips, acid un-productive soils, and general treelessness. But the designated areas show the best of the county, and this it would be hard to surpass anywhere. The north coast offers a succession of rugged cliffs where the force of the Atlantic explores the weaknesses in the contorted slates and sandstones. The south offers deep wooded valleys descending to the sea, sheltered coves, and multi-coloured cliffs. And in the far west the country of West Penwith, the Land's End, there are the pillared granite cliffs and the wind-swept downs littered with the logans, quoits, stone circles and tumuli that go back even to pre-Celtic times.

CENTRES   Bodmin, Bude, Falmouth, Helston, Looe, New-quay, Padstow, Penzance, St Ives

PLACES OF INTEREST   Bedruthan Steps, Boscastle, Brown Willy, Crack-ington Haven, Fowey, Kynance Cove, Lamorna Cove, Land's End, Lizard Point, Mevagissey, Minack Theatre (Porthcurno), Mousehole, Pen-dennis, Polperro, Port Isaac, St Michael's Mount, St Mawes Castle, Tintagel, Zennor

Cotswolds

The Cotswolds was the largest of the conservation areas suggested in the Hobhouse Report, covering about 660 square miles, mostly in Gloucestershire but spreading over into five other counties. The area eventually considered by the National Parks Commission was not quite so large, but the consultations on its 582 square miles involved four county councils—Gloucestershire, Oxfordshire, Worcestershire and Wiltshire—and no fewer than twenty-one district councils. The designation was made and confirmed in 1966.

The area is wedge-shaped, stretching from the Evenlode Valley to the outskirts of Bath. Its north-western boundary is defined by the prominent scarp which overlooks the Vales of Gloucester and Evesham, including a few of the outlying hills and, particularly, the great mass of Bredon Hill. The other long boundary excludes the towns of Malmesbury, Cirencester, Fairford and Lechlade, and follows in places the line of the Roman roads of Fosse Way and Akeman Street. The built-up part of the Stroud gap is excluded.

The Cotswolds are perhaps the best-known part of that broad belt of scarplands that marks the outcrop of the Jurassic rocks from the coast of Dorset north-eastwards to the coast of Yorkshire. The rocks dip gently to the south-east and the higher parts of the area, nearest to the escarpment, are capped by a considerable thickness of limestones and sandstones, which have provided the distinctive building materials of the Cotswold villages. Narrow valleys, mostly following the dip slope, break up the smooth, undulating expanses of the upland plateau, and occasionally cut through to the clays below. Only in two places are there river gaps through the line of the scarp—at Bath where the Avon winds its way through towards Bristol, and at Stroud where the Frome has carved the narrow gorge sometimes known as the Golden Valley.

The high land of the Cotswolds is nowadays an intensively farmed landscape, with its neat stone walls and hedges, fewer sheep but more cattle and arable. Cobbett found it 'an ugly country' and the 'stone brash' soil very shallow, but also noted that the crops, particularly early turnips and winter wheat, had a fair success. Lamenting the decay of the villages in the valleys because of the decline of cottage industry, he remarked that 'the building materials being stone, the ruins do not totally disappear for ages!' He was, however, able to see more prosperity in the Stroud valley: 'a pig in almost every cottage sty; and that is the infallible mark of a happy people.'

Cotswold landscape near Ford, Gloucestershire.

Cotswold architecture: the village of Stanton, Gloucestershire.

The villages of the Cotswolds include many of the most beautiful in Britain, and are as much a part of the attraction of this area as the landscape. The prosperity of the woollen industry, which Cobbett saw on the decline, had in earlier centuries contributed to the building of the fine large churches with their costly monuments and brasses, the spacious streets and market squares of the small towns, and the wealth of substantial stone-built houses. Chipping Campden, in the northern tip of the area, is full of good examples, and has a stylish, arcaded market hall; Castle Combe, in the delightful Bybrook Valley, is one of the best known of the villages. At Bibury, another contender for the 'prettiest village' crown, woollen industry cottages may be seen at Arlington Row, with a communal drying field opposite. There is a fine seventeenth-century mill here, a feature of many of the valley villages, where water-power was an important factor in the industry.

The great limestone escarpment offers the most dramatic scenery of the area, and there are spectacular road descents into the vale below at Birdlip, Crickley, Leckhampton, Winchcombe, Stanway and Broadway. Fine beechwoods cling to the edge in many places and fill the steep bays and combes along the irregular central section of the escarpment. The Cotswolds are considered to be about the westerly limit of natural beechwood, which also occurs in the east-flowing valleys of the dip slope. These woodlands and the limestone plants of the area are of great interest to the naturalist, and there are a number of sites of special scientific importance. At Westonbirt the Arboretum, run by the Forestry Commission, contains some splendid specimen trees.

For other tastes, the area is rich in ancient monuments, tumuli, barrows and some forts, Roman roads and old trackways like Salt Way to explore, and a number of great houses and gardens. Near the village of Guiting Power there is a place of unique interest, the Cotswold Farm Park and rare breed survival centre, where visitors can see something of the history of British livestock breeding.

CENTRES	Bath, Bristol, Cheltenham, Cirencester, Gloucester, Stroud
PLACES OF INTEREST	Badminton House, Bibury (Arlington Mill, Country Museum, and village), Bredon Hill, Buckland Rectory, Castle Combe, Chavenage manor, Chedworth Roman Villa, Chipping Campden, Cleeve Hill, Cotswold Farm Park (near Guiting Power), Dodington House, Dyrham Park, Hailes Abbey (near Stanway), Lasborough Manor, Owlpen Manor, Painswick Court House, Snowshill Manor, Sudeley Castle, Witcombe Roman Villa, Westonbirt Arboretum

Dedham Vale

Dedham Vale is a region of the Stour Valley lying eight miles or so south-west of Ipswich and astride the county boundary of Essex and Suffolk. An area of twenty-two square miles of the Vale became, in 1970, the smallest of the designated areas of outstanding natural beauty, stretching from just west of Manningtree, in Essex, to Nayland in West Suffolk. It is a generally level

The River Stour at Dedham.

and peaceful landscape, consisting mainly of agricultural land, with water meadows, marked hedgerows with many fine elms, scattered woodland and attractive villages.

Despite its small size, this area has had a considerable influence on most people's attitude to English landscape beauty through the paintings of John Constable (1776–1837), and the Vale is widely known as the 'Constable Country'. Born at East Bergholt, just within the area, Constable was the son of a well-to-do miller and intended to follow the family business, but left to study painting in London. Many of his paintings reflect his deep feeling for the countryside along the Stour. 'Painting', he wrote, 'is with me but another word for feeling . . . the sound of water escaping from Mill dams, Willows, old water Banks, slimy posts and brick work . . . made me a painter.' Flatford Mill, Willy Lott's Cottage and the church of Stoke-by-Nayland are recurring subjects in his paintings and sketches, and while much in the Vale has now changed, the beauty and atmosphere of his work can still be recaptured by visitors to the area. Flatford Mill, which belonged to Constable's father, is now owned by the National Trust and used as a Field Studies Council centre.

The designated area is bisected by the A12 road from Colchester to Ipswich which passes through Stratford St Mary. In Constable's day and before, this was a main route from the rich Suffolk pastures to the markets of London. Geese and turkeys as well as cattle passed along the road in huge droves; Defoe calculated that 150,000 turkeys passed over Stratford Bridge every year on their way to London.

During the summer months the area attracts numerous visitors, mostly on day trips, to drive through the picturesque villages and the pleasant pastoral countryside. Considerable portions of the banks of the Stour are now protected by National Trust ownership or covenants which cover over 4000 acres within the designated area.

CENTRES   Colchester, Hadleigh, Ipswich, Sudbury

PLACES OF INTEREST   Castle House (Dedham), Flatford Mill, Stoke-by-Nayland, Willy Lott's Cottage

Dorset

In 1957 nearly 40 per cent of the county of Dorset was designated an area of outstanding natural beauty, making it, at 400 square miles, the third largest in the country. It includes most of the higher land in the county, the chalk downs, sandy heaths and wooded valleys, as well as the entire Dorset coastline except for an area around Portland and Weymouth. The broad band of downland stretches from Pilsdon Pen, overlooking the Axe valley and the borders of Devon, to the valley of the Stour, just by the town of Blandford Forum. Divided from this northern arm by the rich pastoral country of the Trent and Frome valleys, a southern arm, encircling the county town of Dorchester, extends eastwards into the Isle of Purbeck, broadening to take in the greater part of Poole Harbour. There was an early plan to include King John's ancient Royal hunting forest of Cranborne Chase, in the north-east, but this was discarded, as only part of the Chase lies within Dorset.

On the whole the shape of the designated area follows the shape of the extensive chalk mass of Dorset. But the coastline is one of the most varied and fascinating in these islands, displaying fine sections through all the rocks of the Jurassic system from the grey clays and limestones at Lyme Regis, with their abundant ammonites and other fossils, to the famous Portland and Purbeck limestones. With its almost vertically dipping rocks, the Isle of Purbeck resembles the Isle of Wight in structure. At Foreland, north of Swanage, the narrow spine of chalk that forms the Purbeck Hills ends in the Old Harry Rocks, which point towards the Needles across a wide breach that the sea once made to penetrate the Solent and Poole Harbour. Smaller examples of this breaching action can be seen farther west in Purbeck, where the sea has broken through the resistant limestones to scoop out Worbarrow Bay and Lulworth Cove in the softer rocks behind. Chesil Beach, which joins the Isle of Portland (not part of the area) to the mainland, is a unique feature. No one has yet produced a thorough explanation of the remarkable grading of pebbles in this sixteen-mile shingle bank. The pebbles decrease in size from the Portland end westwards, and it is reasonably claimed that smugglers landing on the beach at night could tell where they were by examining them.

A straight Roman road runs south from Dorchester towards Weymouth, passing just to the east of an earlier settlement that the Roman Durnovaria replaced. This is Maiden Castle, the gigantic fortress and hill settlement which is probably the finest Iron Age site in Europe; its grassy ramparts, deep

Looking towards the coast from the ramparts of Eggardon Hill. In the background (centre) is Golden Cap.

ditches and complicated entrance fortifications are in the care of the Department of the Environment. Like so much of the chalk country of southern England, Dorset is rich in earthworks ranging from Stone Age to Romano-British times. The 180-foot club-wielding giant carved on a hillside just north of Cerne Abbas is believed to be a pagan fertility figure; in the last century a small thicket, now happily removed, was grown to cover his unashamed nakedness. Another chalk-cut monument, of much later date, is the white horse on the downs above Weymouth Bay, to which the town of Weymouth added a representation of George III, in thanks for royal patronage. Unfortunately horse and monarch happened to be turning their backs on Weymouth; the king was offended and the town's tribute misfired.

On a second road out of Dorchester, going towards Wareham, and just on the edge of the designated area, is Max Gate, the home of Thomas Hardy from 1885 until his death in 1928. The Wessex countryside of his poems and novels lies all around. 'Egdon Heath', Hardy's birthplace at Higher Bockhampton, and the church at Stinsford where his heart is supposed to be buried (though according to one story it was stolen by a stray cat!) are outside our area, but away north of Cerne the landscape of *The Woodlanders* surrounds Minterne (Great Hintock), now also visited for the fine arboretum and gardens there.

One of many fine viewpoints on the downs and heathland is Black Down, above Portesham, crowned by the monument to that other Thomas Hardy, the captain who served with Nelson. The hill between Swyre and Abbotsbury also has splendid views over Chesil Beach and the Fleet, the narrow lagoon between it and the mainland. At Abbotsbury, thousands visit the famous Swannery, the largest in Europe; it has been part of the Strangeways Estate since Elizabethan times. Poole Harbour, like the Fleet, has great numbers of water-fowl and wading birds. There are nature reserves at Arne, Hartland Heath and Studland, the last of which has a nature trail and hide facilities.

CENTRES	Blandford Forum, Bridport, Dorchester, Lyme Regis, Poole, Swanage, Wareham, Weymouth
PLACES OF INTEREST	Abbotsbury, Blue Pool (near Wareham), Brownsea Island, Cerne Abbas, Corfe Castle, Creech Grange, Durdle Door, Forde Abbey, Golden Cap, Hardy Monument, Lulworth Cove, Maiden Castle, Milton Abbas, Minterne (near Cerne), Parnham House, Studland Dunes, Tilly Whim Caves

East Devon

From the summit of the Golden Cap, looking westwards past Lyme Regis, the first of the red cliffs of Devon can be seen. This western end of Lyme Bay is part of the East Devon area of outstanding natural beauty, designated in 1963. The area, which totals 103 square miles, stretches from the county boundary near Lyme Regis to the outskirts of Exmouth, and inland up to seven miles, just short of Honiton and Axminster. There was an earlier proposal to include the Blackdown Hills, which spill over into Somerset, but

Gittisham village, near Honiton.

this was decided against before actual designation plans were advanced. On the coast small areas around the resorts of Sidmouth, Beer and Seaton are excluded.

Budleigh Salterton is a name known to English geology from the occurrence there of remarkable pebble beds, whose round, waterworn pebbles were laid down something like 200 million years ago. These beds form a small part of a vast series of red marls, sandstones and conglomerates that give to the fields of Devon their characteristic rich red colour. Emerging from beneath the gently east-dipping blue-grey clays and limestones of the Dorset coast, rocks of this series reach the shore near Seaton. Overlying these older rocks and forming the white cliffs of Beer Head, are outliers of the chalk and greensand that cover much of inland Dorset. It is these rocks that have produced the spectacular landslip just east of Lyme, part of which is a national nature reserve. Nearly five miles of cliff have tumbled to the shore here at different times, and the old coast road, fragments of which cling to the cliff edge in some places, was the third to perish in this way. Today the main road goes well inland.

And inland too, this is an area of considerable charm. On the hill above the lace-making town of Honiton, Defoe observed that 'the view of the country is the most beautiful landskip in the world—a meer picture'. Views from East Hill, Gittisham Hill, Aylesbeare Common and Woodbury Common are as fine or finer, the last covering the broad sweep of the Exe estuary. Blackbury Castle, an impressive hill fort and earthworks in the care of the Department of the Environment, three miles north-west of Beer, is another good viewpoint. The coast of the area, rich in good cliff walking, is one of the best stretches of the South Devon Coast Path (see p. 239).

The beach at Budleigh Salterton is the setting of that famous painting by Millais—'The Boyhood of Raleigh'. Hayes Barton, a couple of miles inland, is Sir Walter Raleigh's birthplace, a large thatched house with wings at either end. Not far from there, at Bicton Gardens, are the Italian Gardens laid out in 1735 from designs by Le Notre, architect of the gardens at Versailles.

CENTRES   Axminster, Budleigh Salterton, Exmouth, Honiton, Lyme Regis, Seaton, Sidmouth

PLACES OF INTEREST   Bicton Gardens, Branscombe, Farway Country Park, Hayes Barton, Ladram Bay, The Landslip

East Hampshire

A geologist looking at the plan of designated areas in the south-east of England would instantly recognize in their outline the boundaries of the chalk and greensand outcrop. For the linked areas of East Hampshire, Sussex Downs, Surrey Hills and North Kent Downs coincide quite accurately with the hills and downland that encircle the Weald of Kent and Sussex. The Weald is a remarkable feature: originally an oval dome structure shaped like a pie with the chalk as its crust, it has, over a history of fifty million years, been mostly eaten away. The North and South Downs are the parts of the crust still adhering to the dish, and the filling that remains around the pie-funnel forms the Ashdown Forest.

Looking across the village pond at Buriton.

The area of East Hampshire designated in 1961* forms a natural extension of the South Downs. Covering 161 square miles, from the Sussex-Hampshire border nearly to Winchester, it is an area of chalk downs and rolling farmland, characterized in the north and east by the famous beechwood 'hangers'. Cobbett's description of his approach to Hawkley Hanger is one of the most delightful in his 'Rides': he came, all in a moment, to the very edge of the hanger, pulled up his horse, and sat and looked. 'It was looking from the top of a castle down into the sea, except that the valley was land and not water.' Another hanger, even better known, is that which looks down to Gilbert White's village of Selborne, vividly brought to life in the parson-naturalist's letters.

In more direct line with the Sussex Downs lie Butser Hill, a fine near-900-foot viewpoint, and Old Winchester Hill, where there is a national nature reserve, while beyond these the Meon Valley cuts northwards into the area. Petersfield, in the east, is the principal town, but at St Catherine's Hill, the western limit, one can survey the city of Winchester, old capital of Wessex and county town of Hampshire. The village of Hambledon, in the south, has significance for every cricketer; on Windmill and Broadhalfpenny Downs, above the village, cricket really began to take shape as the national game. In the north can be seen a different sort of battlefield, the remarkably unchanged site of one of those inconclusive Civil War actions, the battle of Alresford or Cheriton. It should perhaps have been a Cavalier victory, but, as Clarendon records, 'the King's horse never behaved themselves so ill as that day' (29th March 1644), and by evening both sides had had enough. Cheriton Wood was the scene of some of the fiercest fighting.

The local planning authority, Hampshire County Council, has, as part of a policy for the area, purchased a number of public open spaces, notably at Ashford Chace and Butser Hill.

* Confirmed in 1962.

CENTRES   Petersfield, Winchester

PLACES OF INTEREST   Ashford Chace, Butser Hill, Cheesefoot Head, Hambledon, Old Winchester Hill, Selborne

Forest of Bowland

Detached from the Pennines by the Valley of the Ribble, the Forest of Bowland is a compact area of similar country—broad, steep-sided gritstone fells
and open moorland rising to over 1800 feet at the highest point. The area of
outstanding natural beauty designated in 1963 and confirmed in 1964 lies
partly in Lancashire and partly in the West Riding of Yorkshire, including
the foothills of the Forest and the detached mass of Pendle Hill in its total of
310 square miles. A large proportion of the area is open country, the high
fells and moorland being used for rough grazing, grouse moor and water
catchment. But there are also attractive dales, such as Hinburndale, Little-
dale, Roeburndale and Swyredale, with good dairy land in their lower reaches.
These and the Hodder, Ribble and Lune valley areas are wooded in places
and have some fine riverside walks.

In the north-east the area adjoins the Yorkshire Dales National Park. The
boundary here is the Craven fault, a giant earth fracture in which the down-
throw to the south takes the mountain limestone far underground again,

The rounded outlines of Bowland seen from Beacon Fell Country Park.

leaving at the surface the newer Millstone Grit of the Bowland Fells. But at the edges of the area, particularly near Clitheroe, can be seen some fine examples of the 'reef knolls', humps of limestone that are thought to derive from coral reefs in the limestone sea of Carboniferous times.

The Forest of Bowland is an area almost without major roads, and the population is scattered, with few large villages. It has thus remained remarkably unspoiled, despite its proximity to the heavily populated regions of Lancashire. Pressure is mostly confined to a few areas, particularly Pendle, Longridge Fell and the Trough of Bowland, and along the A683 road in the north-west. On the fells the areas with footpaths are few in number, but are well used, while the lowland footpaths along the banks of the Lune near Caton in the north-west or around Brock Mill in the south-west are also popular. At Beacon Fell, on the southern edge of the area, one of the country's first country parks was established, with good car access, walks and viewpoints. Roads such as that over the Nick of Pendle, from which there are good views, or through the Trough of Bowland, tend to get badly overcrowded on summer Sundays.

Many visitors will want to climb Pendle Hill, which can be done from Barley by a well-marked track or from Downham, a picturesque stone village with Norman church and a village green on which the stocks still stand. Not only is the hill notorious as a haunt of witches, it is famous as the site of a vision. In 1652 George Fox was impelled to climb to the summit, from which he saw a great people to be gathered. On his descent he preached to many groups in the area, often in the open air, and formed the nucleus of the Quaker movement. There are still many old meeting-houses in the surrounding villages, and Quakerism is still strong throughout North Lancashire and Westmorland, a region known to Quakers as 'the 1652 country'.

CENTRES	Clitheroe, Lancaster, Preston
PLACES OF INTEREST	Beacon Fell Country Park, Brock Mill, Browsholme Hall, Crook o' Lune (Caton), Pendle Hill, Trough of Bowland

Gower

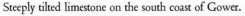

Gower was the first 'area of outstanding natural beauty' to be designated. By the end of 1955 the National Parks Commission had completed work on all ten of the present national parks, and felt able to turn their attention to this other form of designation. Gower they considered an area of particular importance because of its proximity to densely populated areas of South Wales, for whose inhabitants it had long been a popular retreat, and because it had, they knew, been under threat of undesirable or doubtful development. In that year, therefore, they opened consultations with Glamorgan and Swansea, the two local planning authorities involved, and in 1956 the designation of seventy-three square miles of Gower was made and confirmed.

An area of classic coastal scenery, the Gower is an example of an old plain of marine erosion, a feature common round the edge of Wales. In this case the

Steeply tilted limestone on the south coast of Gower.

sea of earlier times, at levels 200 feet and 400 feet above its present level relative to the land, cut right across an area of sharply folded rocks. Some indication of what lies underneath the plateau of Gower can be seen, not only in the cliffs, but in the ridges of Cefn Bryn, Rhossili Down and Llanmadoc Hill where Old Red Sandstone rocks, folded up from below, resisted erosion. The dominant rock is the Carboniferous limestone of the southern cliffs from Mumbles Head to Worms Head. On the plateau of Gower it is often disguised beneath glacial deposits, but there are several limestone valleys, reminiscent of examples elsewhere from the Mendips to Derbyshire, with crags and wooded slopes. Sandy bays and coves add to the attractions of the coastline. The northern shoreline of the peninsula is formed by the estuary of the Loughor, where sand and marsh have left stranded the old shoreline on which stand Cheriton, Llanrhidian and Weobley Castle.

Though on Swansea's doorstep, Gower has managed to preserve much of its isolation. There are no through roads, no major settlements and, cut off from Welsh Glamorgan by the ridge of Coal Measure sandstone across its neck, the peninsula has, like South Pembrokeshire, preserved a little of the England the Normans brought into Wales. Norman castles were at Penrice, Scurlage near Llandewi, and Weobley, where their ruins may still be seen.

There are two important national nature reserves on Gower. Worms Head, where the level of the old wave-cut platform can be clearly seen, is a long island joined to the mainland at low tide, and has rich plant and bird life. At Oxwich, a large reserve of 542 acres contains great variety of habitat from sand dunes to scrub woodland. A Sand Trail for visitors, gently educating them in their effect on a sensitive sand dune system, has been laid out, and there is a Gower Countryside Centre in the Old School at Oxwich.

CENTRE   Swansea

PLACES OF INTEREST   Arthur's Stone, Mumbles, Oxwich, Parc Le Breos (burial chamber), Penrice Castle, Port Eynon, Rhossili Bay, Weobley Castle, Worms Head

Isle of Wight

The shape of the Isle of Wight is familiar to anyone who can draw even the roughest map of England, a diamond shape with its longer axis running east to west. The island is, as Dudley Stamp has said, a geological museum, as interesting in its structure as in its strata. A sharp upfold of chalk forms the ridge of downland from Foreland in the east to the Needles in the west, almost vertical there and at Alum Bay. The younger rocks north of the ridge dip gently towards the more sheltered coastline of the Solent, while to the south lie the older clays and sands folded over so that a second area of chalk downland with only a gentle dip to the south is produced. This broader area of chalk gives the highest land in the island at St Boniface Down (785 feet) above Ventnor.

An area of seventy-three square miles of the Island was designated in 1963, including most of the central ridge from Newport west to the Needles and east to Culver Cliff and Foreland, and extending northwards to Wootton Bridge in its eastern section and along the valley of the Yar in the west to take in the ferry port of Yarmouth. The southern downs from Luccombe to Niton are joined at St Catherine's Point to a broad triangular area stretching north to Newport and west to Freshwater, and stretches of the Solent coast from Yarmouth to Gurnard and from East Cowes to Quarr include in the area most of the unspoiled coastline of the Island.

The Romans knew Vectis as one of the more tolerable spots of this corner of their Empire, a place to build villas, but the remains of these are easily outnumbered by the tumuli, barrows and field systems of earlier inhabitants living on the chalklands above the more wooded tracts to north and south. Up to much more recent times the island was quite well wooded: in the time of Charles II, it is said, 'a squirrel might travel on the tops of trees for many leagues together'. The needs of Portsmouth dockyard, not far away, much reduced the forest over the next century.

There is much to see within the designated area. From the resort of Ventnor westwards lies an impressive landslip known as the Undercliff extending as far as Blackgang Chine. The chines are deep ravines dropping to the beach through the greensand and Wealden beds, and they provide access at several points from the old military road which runs just inland from Blackgang to Brook. Just beyond lies Freshwater, and the house to which Tennyson retired. A monument stands on the Down that bears his name and on which he must have walked, perhaps recalling the feeling underfoot of his own native wolds

Compton Bay looking east.

in Lincolnshire. Another place of retirement, on the other side of the Island, is Osborne House, a favourite residence of Queen Victoria, and a less comfortable royal retreat is to be found at Carisbrooke Castle, near Newport, once the prison of Charles I. A less visited spot is the once-busy port of Newtown, originally called Francheville and, until the 1800s, capable of taking ships of 500 tons or more. This was a classic 'rotten borough'; at one time thirty-three voters returned two members to parliament. The seventeenth-century manor house at Arreton, and Nunwell House near Brading, held in one family for 450 years, are both well worth visiting.

CENTRES — Cowes, Newport, Ryde, Sandown, Shanklin, Ventnor

PLACES OF INTEREST — Alum Bay, Arreton Manor, Blackgang Chine, Carisbrooke Castle, Freshwater Down, Newtown, Nunwell House, Osborne, Quarr Abbey, Yarmouth Castle

Kent Downs

The white cliffs of Dover are probably the best-known feature of England's chalk country. When the Kent Downs were designated in 1968 they became the eastern limit of a vast tract of designated territory extending west nearly to Winchester and back along the South Downs to Eastbourne. The Kent Downs area adjoins the Surrey Hills area near Westerham and, from only just outside Orpington and the London suburbs, stretches in a widening ribbon of rolling countryside some sixty miles to the coast. There it takes in the cliffs of South Foreland as a small outlier to the area, and includes Shakespeare Cliff, Folkestone Warren, and a narrow strip of the old sea cliff west of Hythe, overlooking Romney Marsh. Inland the Downs rise to 600 feet, giving fine views over the Weald of Kent. The total area designated is 326 square miles.

This ribbon of land follows roughly the outcrop of the chalk and green-sand. As Cobbett was sharp enough to observe, the 'chalk-ridge' and the 'sand-ridge' run parallel to each other all the way from Farnham to the Straits of Dover, where he could see them in cross-section as sand and chalk cliffs. The well-jointed chalk forms steep cliffs, except where, as at Folkestone Warren, the blue Gault Clay is at beach level and has caused massive land-slips seawards.

As the part of England nearest to the continent of Europe, the coastline within the area is studded with defensive structures. The more modern of these are regarded as eyesores, but they only form part of a pattern that goes back to Roman times. Dover has its castle, with a massive twelfth-century keep and within the curtain walls the remains of a Roman lighthouse. Just beyond Hythe, at Lympne, are the remains of Stutfall Castle, or Lemanis, a Fort of the Saxon Shore with walls over twelve feet thick, while not far from it lies a much later fortification, the Royal Military Canal. Of this, as of the nearby Martello Towers, Cobbett was particularly scornful: 'those armies who had so often crossed the Rhine and the Danube were to be kept back by a canal, made by Pitt, thirty feet wide at the most!' he wrote, appalled at the extravagance of defence expenditure.

The pleasant countryside of Kent has always attracted settlement. From the Roman Villa at Lullingstone to the elegant William and Mary manor of Squerrye's Court near Westerham, the designated area is well endowed with fine historic houses. The largest, and indeed one of the largest in England, is Knole, near Sevenoaks, with its splendid State Rooms, Jacobean furniture and

Wrotham Hill and the view over the orchard county of Kent.

171

silver. But many of the smaller houses such as Ightham Mote, Quebec House at Westerham, and Owletts at Cobham have a great deal of interest.

The North Downs Way (see p. 213) threads its way through the area, keeping to the crest of the downs. On its line, just north-east of Ashford, lies a national nature reserve at Crundale Downs, near Wye, which is a fine example of a chalkland habitat.

CENTRES   Ashford, Canterbury, Dover, Faversham, Folkestone, Hythe, Maidstone, Rochester, Sevenoaks, Westerham

PLACES OF INTEREST   Chartwell, Chilham, Cobham, Dover Castle, Eynsford Castle, Folkestone Warren, Ightham Mote, Knole, Lullingstone Castle, Lullingstone Roman Villa, Lympne Castle, Owletts (Cobham), Quebec House (Westerham), Shakespeare Cliff (Dover), Squerrye's Court (Westerham), Stutfall Castle (Lympne), Wrotham Hill

Lleyn

Westwards from the mountains of Snowdonia stretches the long peninsula of Lleyn, a land of quite different character from the rest of Caernarvonshire. Inland it is a countryside of narrow lanes, turf banks, dazzling white cottages of a chunky appearance, rough meadows, gorse and bracken. But the main attraction is the coastline, a succession of rocky headlands, tiny hidden harbours and broad sandy beaches. The Welsh words *porth* (bay or harbour), *traeth* (beach), *pen* (headland), *ynys* (island) and *carreg* (rock) constantly recur, for this isolated country is a Welsh-speaking stronghold, where English is definitely the second language. In 1956 most of the coast of the peninsula was included in what was the third area of outstanding natural beauty to be designated, a total of sixty square miles, divided narrowly into two by the resorts of Nefyn and Morfa Nefyn. The designation was confirmed in May 1957.

The generally level nature of the peninsula, with the hills standing out like islands, is, like the platform of Anglesey, the result of marine erosion. The

Bardsey Island and the coast of Lleyn from near Rhiw.

sea cut back its shores into the old rocks giving a level sea floor which has now been left high and dry by subsequent change in the levels of land and sea. The hills, notably Yr Eifl, a trio of peaks rising to 1849 feet, are in fact one time rocky islands. The resistant rocks of this group have attracted some quarrying, formerly more extensive than now, for a deserted quarrying village and quay lie at the foot of a steep road from Llithfaen, at Porth y Nant.

Either of the two main routes down to the end of the peninsula, from Caernarvon through Nefyn, Tudweiliog and Llangwnadl on the north side, or from Pwllheli through Llanbedrog and on the B4413, or better, along the precipitous road through Rhiw if it is open, will give some idea of the lie of the land, but the coastline is best explored on foot. Car access points tend to fill quickly during the summer. At the tip of Lleyn, however, a concrete road winds its way to the summit of Mynydd Mawr and gives access to the National Trust land at Braich y Pwll, where this Land's End of Wales slopes steeply into the sea. Across the Sound lies Bardsey Island, formerly a place of pilgrimage. Its monastery is now in ruins, but the island is an important bird observatory. It can be reached from the little port of Aberdaron, once the embarkation point of the pilgrims, whose ancient *cegin* (kitchen) now serves teas.

Settlements of any size are few on the peninsula. But Llanbedrog, with its sheltered position, is popular for holidays, and Abersoch has become a smart sailing resort. Many of the beaches have kept free from the paraphernalia of exploitation because of their isolated position. Most offer good bathing, though the $3\frac{1}{2}$ miles of Porth Neigwl or Hell's Mouth are notorious for dangerous offshore currents. Porth Oer on the northern coast is remarkable for the sound given by its sands when they are walked on; its other name is Whistling Sands.

The area has a number of important sites for the naturalist. Besides Bardsey, the Gwylan Islands and St Tudwal's Islands are seabird sanctuaries, and the latter has a seal colony. On the north coast are several sites of geological and marine biological interest. For the archaeologist too this is a rich area, with standing stones and burial chambers, while for any visitor a climb from the road to the impressive hill fort and settlement of Tre'r Ceiri on Yr Eifl is worth while. Finally the one inland extension of the area should not be neglected; the valley of the River Horon running through it is a quite different, but equally attractive, kind of landscape.

CENTRES   Aberdaron, Abersoch, Nevin, Pwllheli

PLACES OF INTEREST   Bardsey Island, Braich y Pwll, Llanbedrog, Porth Dinllaen, Porth Oer, Plas yn Rhiw, Tre'r Ceiri, Yr Eifl (The Rivals)

Malvern Hills

'From Bredon Hill', wrote Cobbett, riding into Worcestershire, 'those curious bubblings-up, the Malvern Hills, are right before you, and only at about ten miles distance, in a straight line.' Some of the oldest rocks in England bubbled up to form the Malvern Hills, which rise like a barrier alongside the Severn plain just southwest of Worcester. These pre-Cambrian rocks, granite-like in their hardness, form the core of the north-south ridge. Although the hills are not high—the highest, Worcestershire Beacon, being not quite 1400 feet—their abruptness makes them one of the most prominent features of the Midlands. The views eastward, from the steep fault-scarp, are staggering. Spread out below is the Vale of Severn in a twenty-mile panorama, across which one can often see a procession of weather passing, storm-clouds and sunshine. Beyond lies the mass of Bredon Hill and the long line of the Cotswold escarpment.

A rider enjoying winter sunshine on the slopes of the Malvern Hills.

These magnificent hills are part of an area of forty square miles in the counties of Gloucestershire, Herefordshire and Worcestershire, designated in October 1959. It stretches from Knightwick in the north to Bromsberrow in the south, bounded on the west by the villages of Suckley, Cradley, Coddington and Wellington Heath, and the outskirts of Ledbury, while on the east it takes in Malvern Wells and West Malvern, which cling to the steep slope of the hills, and skirts the resort of Great Malvern.

Hill-forts, earthworks and trackways along the hills are evidence of the importance of the range to earlier ages, and their defence role continued in more recent times with the warning beacons on the highest summits. The bare appearance of the hills has probably changed little since the fourteenth century when the author of *Piers Plowman* looked to the east, right into the sun, and saw his elaborate vision of 'a field full of folk'. But the hills have musical, as well as literary associations; the half-heard song of a group of Welsh singers on the slopes was part of the inspiration of Elgar's *Introduction and Allegro,* and from his youth the composer had a deep affection for the Malverns, easily visible from his birthplace at Broad Heath, near Worcester.

North to south, the main heights are North Hill (1307 feet), Worcestershire Beacon (1394) feet, Herefordshire Beacon (1114 feet) and Midsummer Hill (937 feet), the last owned by the National Trust. The hills are deceptively steep, and people often arrive at British Camp (Herefordshire Beacon) exhausted, having been misled into thinking the direct route the quickest. But one could walk for weeks on the diagonal paths that criss-cross the slopes without covering the same path twice.

CENTRES   Great Malvern, Ledbury, Worcester

PLACES OF INTEREST   Alfrick (Nature Reserve), British Camp, Eastnor Castle, Midsummer Hill, St Ann's Well, Worcestershire Beacon

Mendip Hills

Among the most recently designated of the areas of outstanding natural beauty are the Mendip Hills. The area designated comprises more than half of the Mendips, stretching from Bleadon Hill in the west, only two miles from Weston Bay, eastwards as far as the A39 road from Bath to Wells. In its north-east corner is Chew Magna Lake, and the boundary extends southwards from there to the foot of the Mendip scarp above the cathedral city of Wells, then following the scarp westwards past Cheddar Gorge back

Burrington Combe, one of the dry gorges cut into the edge of Mendip.

to Bleadon Hill. The northern boundary takes in Blagdon Lake but omits an area of low-lying land around Winscombe and Shipham where residential development is taking place.

The bulk of Mendip is made up by a great plateau of Carboniferous Limestone rising to over 1000 feet at Blackdown. Here and at Bleadon Hill there are fine views over the Bristol Channel and the surrounding countryside. Eastwards from the latter viewpoint can be seen the steeply dipping limestone promontory of Brean Down and, beyond, yet another extension of Mendip in Steep Holm, three miles out in the Channel.

With its short turf, grey limestone walls and lack of trees, the plateau landscape resembles that of other mountain limestone areas. Underground streams have dissolved the rock away to give several cave systems, in some of which traces of occupation by man in prehistoric times have been found. Wookey Hole and Cheddar Caves are nationally famous and both have spectacular stalactite formations. Cheddar Gorge, a narrow chasm cut into the dipping rocks of the Mendip edge, is now largely dry, its watercourse having sunk below ground.

Traces of man's occupation of the Mendips can be seen at many places on the plateau. The Nine Barrows on Priddy Hill are of Bronze Age and the impressive hill fort of Dolebury on its steeply sloping site is Iron Age. From Iron Age times until the eighteenth century Mendip was well known as a mining area, lead and, later, zinc being the two most valuable metals. Traces of the industry still remain, but today quarrying is more important, and its extension threatens some parts of the area.

With the M5 motorway pushing west from Bristol, the Mendips, which are already well used for outdoor recreation, will become still more accessible. Walking and riding over the old droving routes and 'green roads' that cross the plateau are popular, and several caving clubs are trying to find extensions to the twenty-two miles of caves already known underground. There are nature trails at Wells, Long Wood and Ebbor Gorge, the last-named site being a national nature reserve.

CENTRES   Cheddar, Wells, Weston-super-Mare

PLACES OF INTEREST   Burrington Combe, Cheddar Gorge, Chew Valley, Ebbor Gorge, Wookey Hole

Norfolk Coast

A fine range of coastal scenery, including cliffs, sand dunes, shingle ridges, salt marsh and mud flats, is the basis of the Norfolk Coast area of outstanding natural beauty. The area of 174 square miles covers about two-thirds of the coast of the county, extending in a strip three to five miles in depth from Hunstanton to Bacton with further stretches on the Wash coast north of King's Lynn and in the east between Sea Palling and Winterton-on-Sea. It was designated in 1967, confirmed the following year.

The Wash coastline is an area where the land is gaining on the sea. There are extensive silt and sand flats exposed at low tide, and land reclamation in the area is producing fine silt soils like those of the neighbouring fens. Inland, the designated area takes in part of the Sandringham Estate, including Sandringham House. Hunstanton, where the cliffs of chalk, red chalk and green-

Blakeney Quay.

sand reach a height of seventy feet, marks the start of the long, continuous central section of the area.

The marshland coast between Holme-next-the-Sea and Weybourne is reckoned the finest of its kind in Britain and probably in Europe. Behind wide beaches and sand or shingle ridges lie salt marsh and reclaimed pastures backed by low hills and intersected by a series of natural creeks and harbours. Brancaster, Burnham Overy, Wells and Blakeney are the best known, providing sheltered waters for sailing and boating. Scolt Head Island is a detached sand barrier now a national nature reserve and famous for its birds, particularly the colonies of Common and Sandwich Terns. Another national nature reserve is at Holkham, where a past reclamation scheme is marked by a belt of Corsican Pines, preventing wind erosion. Blakeney Point is a shingle spit building up from east to west, the main direction of drift along the coast, and there is a fine shingle ridge from Cley to Weybourne. Beaches, shingle, sand, dunes and marshes are constantly shifting and changing, making the whole area a first-class laboratory for the study of coastal evolution.

Beyond Weybourne the coastline is different, for here the sea is gaining on the land. The cliffs of boulder clay, with much chalk, reach over 200 feet in height at Trimmingham, but are being worn away at a rate of several feet a year in many places. The built-up part of the holiday resorts of Sheringham, Cromer and Mundesley are excluded from the designated area, which extends eastwards to just short of the North Sea gas terminal at Bacton. Part of the Cromer Ridge, a moraine pushed up by Ice Age glaciers, lies within the area, and rising to over 300 feet, provides some good views over the neighbouring coast and countryside. In the strip of coast between Sea Palling and Winterton is a third national nature reserve at Winterton Dunes, the largest mainland dune system on the East Anglian coast.

CENTRES   Cromer, Hunstanton, King's Lynn, Mundesley, Sheringham, Wells-next-the-Sea

PLACES OF INTEREST   Blakeney, Brancaster, Burnham Overy, Castle Rising, Holkham Park, Horsey, Overy Staithe, Roman Camp (West Runton), Sandringham (grounds), Scolt Head Island, Winterton Dunes

North Devon

Herculis Promontorium, the Headland of Hercules, was the name given to Hartland Point by the Romans, and certainly this rugged coast with its contorted rocks facing the force of the Atlantic gives an immediate impression of giant elemental strength. In 1959 the whole of the North Devon coast between Marsland Mouth on the Cornish frontier and the boundary of the Exmoor National Park just beyond Combe Martin, with the exception only of the built-up area of Ilfracombe, was designated an area of outstanding natural beauty. It does indeed contain a great deal more natural beauty than most, for over much of its sixty-six square miles it is a landscape of sea, rock and sand. The designation was confirmed in May 1960.

At the eastern end of the area the rocks continue the pattern of the Exmoor coastline. Dipping so steeply southwards as to form hogsback cliffs in some places, they form a more varied coastline, however, because the Ilfracombe

The sharply folded rocks of the Atlantic coast at Hartland Quay.

beds, which reach the shore in Combe Martin Bay, are less resistant than the gritstones to the east. Small valleys which ran parallel to the coast have been invaded by the sea, as at Watermouth. But beyond Ilfracombe where the coastline turns southwards, the grain of the country is end-on to the long Atlantic waves, which have excavated the three-mile bay at Woolacombe between the hard slates of Morte Point and the rocks of Baggy Point. The broad bay of Barnstaple, fronted by sand dunes and a pebble ridge, represents a much larger excavation, for here the hard Devonian rocks have dipped beneath a new series of rocks, comparable in age with the Carboniferous Limestone and Coal Measures found elsewhere in England. It is these rocks—mostly shales and sandstones—which make up the rest of the coast of the area. The sharp folding of the rocks is best seen from Hartland Point southwards where the sea again cuts across the strike of the rocks. There are several waterfalls along this stretch of cliffs where small valleys have been left hanging by the more rapid erosion of the coastline.

Some of the west country's finest beaches lie in this North Devon area. At Woolacombe, Saunton and Westward Ho! surfing is popular, while some of the smaller bays and coves are rich in the Atlantic coast sea shells. At Braunton Burrows the impressive sand dunes from 50 to 100 feet high form a national nature reserve, and there is a site of special scientific interest at the Hobby, near Clovelly, with its steep oak woods. Clovelly itself is famous for its stepped main street which has to be negotiated by foot or by donkey; the village is so tightly hung about its combe that it gets easily crowded, and is best appreciated outside the popular holiday months.

CENTRES   Bideford, Braunton, Ilfracombe, Westward Ho!

PLACES OF INTEREST   Braunton and Northam Burrows, Bucks Mills, Chambercombe Manor, Combe Martin, Clovelly, Hartland Point, Hartland Quay, Watermouth, Woolacombe Sands

Northumberland Coast

'A long coasting county' was Defoe's description of Northumberland, and it is a narrow forty-three mile strip of this coast that became, in 1958, the sixth area of outstanding natural beauty to be designated. The area, a total of fifty square miles, stretches from Amble on the Coquet almost to the Tweed at Berwick, and includes Holy Island and the Farne Islands. Its remoteness from centres of population has always kept it uncrowded, despite the obvious attractions of the broad sandy bays, low cliffs, small fishing villages, and spectacular castles.

The sandstones, limestones and softer beds that make up the coastal plain of the county dip gently towards the sea, giving the coast its low relief. Wide bays are separated by headlands formed from the harder bands of rock or from the Whin Sill. Wherever it occurs in Northumberland, the hard basalt of the Whin Sill creates the dominant features of the landscape. Here it forms the magnificent rock platforms crowned by Bamburgh and Dunstanburgh Castles, the craggy coast around the little port of Craster, the Farne Islands and Holy Island itself.

In the year 635 the devout King Oswald granted the island of Lindisfarne to Bishop Aidan as his see and as a base for missionary activity in the kingdom of Northumbria. From here came the Lindisfarne Gospels, a series of brilliantly intricate decorated manuscripts of the early eighth century. Just as in those times, the island is reached between tides from the mainland by a road over the sands. There is on it a small village, a sixteenth-century castle and the ruins of Lindisfarne Priory (eleventh century).

The sands over which the road to Holy Island passes are part of an extensive nature reserve noted for its many species of wildfowl and wading birds. The Farne Islands (National Trust), which may be visited from Seahouses on the mainland by boats leaving twice daily, are not a national nature reserve, though known internationally for their seabirds and for the grey seal colony. The seals have in recent years become so numerous that they have outgrown their breeding space and, despite protests from well-meaning but uninformed animal-lovers, culls have to be arranged. There is, of course, also support from the local fishing industry for control of the seals, which can do much damage to nets. Besides the salmon fisheries and the seine-net fishing from Seahouses, lobster and crab abound, particularly on the rocky ledges near Craster, a port also famous for its kippers.

A special committee of Northumberland County Council looks after the

Bamburgh Castle, where the hard rock of the Whin Sill reaches the sea.

planning of the area (and of the Northumberland National Park). As guardians of a fine, unspoilt stretch of coastline, the committee are careful to control caravan and chalet development, which has been concentrated in a few locations only.

CENTRES Amble, Alnwick, Alnmouth, Berwick, Bamburgh, Seahouses, Warkworth

PLACES OF INTEREST Bamburgh Castle, Beadnell, Craster, Dunstanburgh Castle, Lindisfarne (Holy Island: Castle and Priory), Farne Islands, Howick Gardens, Seahouses

184

North Wessex Downs

North Wessex Downs is the invented name for a large upland area in Hampshire, Wiltshire and Berkshire, which includes the Marlborough, Lambourn and part of the North Hampshire Downs. At 671 square miles it is now the largest area of outstanding natural beauty designated, larger in fact than all but three of the national parks. Almost encircling Newbury, it is ringed by Reading, Basingstoke, Andover, Devizes, Calne, Swindon and Wantage, extending eastward from the old Civil War battlefield of Roundway Hill, between Calne and Devizes, to the boundary of the Chilterns area at the Goring Gap. To the north it follows the line of downs overlooking the Vale of the White Horse; in the south it is intersected by the Kennet Valley, the Vale of Pewsey and Enbourne Vale, with Savernake Forest between. The Test Valley forms, together with Salisbury Plain, the southern limit of the area.

The area is considered by many to be the largest and least spoiled tract of chalk downland country in southern England, and it has some notable escarpments in the west and above the Vale of Pewsey, the latter rising to 964 feet at Milk Hill. Inkpen Beacon, another ten feet higher, is the highest hill in the area, and stands across the valley farther to the east. On Fyfield Down, three miles north-west of Marlborough, is a classic tract of unreclaimed chalk downland, now a national nature reserve. It is a good place to see examples of the Sarsen or grey wether stones that occur scattered over the downs throughout the area. They are derived from the resistant remains of younger rocks than the chalk now eroded from the area.

The Sarsen stones have been a valuable material for the stone circles, barrows and burial chambers which are found in great numbers on these chalklands. Over a long period of time the downs, because of their freedom from forest, were the most habitable regions in the south. At Avebury is one of the most important Bronze Age monuments in Europe, and nearby Windmill Hill is a site which has given its name to a culture. The massive man-made mound of Silbury Hill, which stands beside the Bath road between Marlborough and Calne, has been excavated but has yet to yield its secrets.

The area also contains a famous battle site of Saxon times. At the battle of Ashdown, Ethelred, King of Wessex, and Alfred his brother (later the Great) inflicted the first major defeat on the Danes and started to turn the tide for their struggling kingdom. The exact battlefield is not easy to find, but the ancient Ridgeway along which the Saxons moved their forces can be followed

Handsome beeches grace Savernake Forest, south-east of Marlborough.

from Goring westward to Lowbury Hill, which was their main defensive position. The Ridgeway, proposed as a long-distance bridleway, passes right through the area, past Uffington Castle and the White Horse on the Berkshire Downs, to curve south over Hackpen Hill and meet the Wansdyke not far from Milk Hill.

As well as having on its borders the expanding towns of Swindon, Reading, Basingstoke and Andover, the area is bisected by the M4, bringing London, Birmingham and Bristol within two hours' travelling time. Parts of the area are already popular for a variety of open-air pursuits, and the three county councils concerned in its planning aim to work out positive measures to protect its beauty.

CENTRES   Andover, Devizes, Marlborough, Newbury, Reading, Swindon

PLACES OF INTEREST   Ashbury (Wayland's Smithy), Ashdown (Alfred's Castle), Ashdown House, Avebury (stone circles, museum), Avebury Manor, Donnington Castle (Newbury), Fyfield Down, Inkpen Beacon, Littlecote House, Pewsey Down, Roundway Down, Sandham Memorial Chapel, Silbury Hill, Uffington (Castle, White Horse), West Kennet Long Barrow

Quantock Hills

In 1956 the Quantock Hills became the first designation of an area of out-standing natural beauty in England (Wales was earlier with the Gower). The Quantocks had originally been proposed for designation as part of the Exmoor National Park, but they are separated from the rather similar sand-stone hills of Exmoor by a tract of land that could not be deemed of national park quality. The thirty-eight square miles of the Quantocks area stretch from the edge of the Vale of Taunton Dene north-west to the sea at Bridgwater Bay,

Will's Neck, the highest point of the Quantocks, stands just above the village of Crowcombe.

in a band about three miles wide in most places. It is a country of smooth hills, bracken-clad slopes, wooded combes and valleys, with a number of picturesque villages.

In 1797 William and Dorothy Wordsworth, who had been living at Racedown in Dorset, moved to Alfoxton, by Holford, so as to be near to their friend Coleridge at Nether Stowey. It was an important move, for the conjunction of the two poets produced, in one year, the *Lyrical Ballads* and the *Rime of the Ancient Mariner*. As Dorothy's delightful journal of their stay at Alfoxton shows, the three were often out walking, in all weathers, over the hills and between their villages. She records her deep feelings for the colours and qualities of the landscape, not hesitating to disentangle them from the picturesque. Of Crookham (Crowcombe) Park she writes: 'Walked about the Squire's grounds. Quaint waterfalls about, about which Nature was very successfully striving to make beautiful what art had deformed—ruins, hermitages etc. . . . Happily we cannot shape the huge hills, or carve out the valleys according to our fancy.'

Coleridge's cottage, owned by the National Trust, is just outside the designated area, but from the village of Holford one can climb uphill by Willoughby Cleeve to the viewpoint of Longstone Hill, again both National Trust properties, along paths that must have been familiar to the Wordsworths. Another good viewpoint is at Quantoxhead, where the hills come down to the sea. Will's Neck (1261 feet) is the highest point of the Quantocks and stands just above the village of Crowcombe, from which it can be reached by way of wooded Triscombe.

There is fine walking country along the whole of the ridge of hills. In the southern part of the area there is more scattered woodland, and red deer, linked to the Exmoor herds, are more likely to be seen in this region. Stags are hunted by the Quantock Staghounds from August to late autumn, when a spell of hind hunting follows.

CENTRES   Bridgwater, Taunton, Watchet

PLACES OF INTEREST   Cothelstone Manor and Gatehouse, Crowcombe Park, Holford (and Alfoxton), Quantoxhead, Timbercombe, Will's Neck

Shropshire Hills

The A49 road from Hereford to Shrewsbury runs parallel to the Welsh border and a dozen or more miles from that earlier boundary line, Offa's Dyke. North of the rich red and green farmland of Herefordshire, and just after leaving Ludlow, it approaches a fascinating region of south Shropshire, where almost parallel hills and valleys run with the strike of the rocks, roughly south-west to north-east. The 300-square-mile Shropshire Hills area of outstanding natural beauty, designated in 1958 and confirmed the following year, sprawls across this stretch of country taking in its best features. Westwards it extends to Clun Forest and the boundary of Radnorshire, north-west to the boundary of Montgomeryshire beyond the Stiperstones, and to the south-east as far as the Clee Hills, while in the north-east it points in a long finger from Wenlock Edge to the Wrekin and Ercall Hills.

The valley of Church Stretton lies almost in the centre of the area, and the road runs through it. On the left is a steep-sided moorland tract, the Longmynd, formed from ancient Pre-Cambrian slates and grits; on the right a line of equally steep hills is formed by tough volcanic rocks of similar age. These hills form excellent viewpoints from which to survey the interesting country on either side. The Valley below is a rift, into which have been dropped the younger shales and limestones whose main outcrop can be seen farther east in the long even line of Wenlock Edge. The intervening country around Hope Bowdler is undulating but its underlying Cambrian and Ordovician rocks dip beneath the shales of Ape Dale at the foot of the Edge. Far off to the north-east the Wrekin stands out as the last outlier of the volcanic rock of Ragleth, Caer Caradoc and the Lawley hills, while away to the south-east can be seen the massive Clee Hills, formed of much younger rocks which have been protected from erosion by a capping of hard basalt.

It is easy to see why Church Stretton is a well-known area to geologists, but there are, in the surrounding countryside, spectacular viewpoints, hill walks, ancient monuments, castles and fine houses to visit, and enough variety to suit all tastes. The Offa's Dyke long-distance footpath (see p. 216) cuts across the Clun area in the south-west, with some of the best stretches of the Dyke on view, as at Spoad Hill, three miles west of the little town of Clun with its ruined castle. Ancient roads lead up on to the plateau of the Longmynd, and to the west lie further rough ridges, including the craggy Stiperstones rising to 1731 feet. Over 4500 acres of the Longmynd moorland, including some $2\frac{1}{2}$ miles of the Portway, belong to the National Trust.

Looking across the farmland of the rift valley near Church Stretton towards the prominent hill of Caer Caradoc.

The country in the east of the area, around Wenlock Edge, is that of Housman's *Shropshire Lad*. Here can be seen the Tudor and Elizabethan manor houses of Plaish Hall, Shipton Hall and Wilderhope, while at Aston Munslow is a building of earlier date with the old timber cruck frame at the White House, where there is also a museum of domestic and agricultural implements and tools. Just within the southern boundary of the area, near Craven Arms, stands Stokesay Castle, one of the oldest and finest moated and fortified houses in Britain.

CENTRES   Church Stretton, Craven Arms, Knighton, Ludlow, Shrewsbury, Wellington

PLACES OF INTEREST   Buildwas Abbey, Caer Caradoc, Chirbury (Mitchell's Fold stone circle), Clee Hill, Clun Castle, Longmynd, Munslow Aston (White House, country museum), Norton Camp, Plaish Hall, Shipton Hall, Stiperstones, Stokesay Castle, Wenlock Edge, Wilderhope Manor, Wrekin

191

Solway Coast

In 1307 Edward I, 'Hammer of the Scots', on his way to Scotland again, died in camp at Burgh Sands, about six miles north-west of the city of Carlisle and considerably less than that from the Border. A seventeenth-century monu-ment marks the supposed spot, looking out across Burgh and Rockcliffe Marshes to Gretna and the Scottish shore of the Solway Firth. From the whole of the open country along the English shore the views of the hills of Dumfries and Kirkcudbright, notably Criffel (1866 feet) are very much part of the beauty and attraction of the forty-one square miles of the Solway Coast desig-nated in 1964.

The area includes thirty-seven miles of coastline between the mouth of the Esk opposite Gretna and the outskirts of Maryport, but excludes the resort of Silloth and a short built-up stretch just north of it. Caravans, often an intru-sion on this kind of coast, are mainly concentrated on this break in the area, where a disused airfield provided a good site. Access to the shore by footpath and bridleway from the coast road that runs almost the full length of the designated area is generally good. A large part of the shore at Burgh Marsh, Cardurnock and Whitrigg at the mouth of the Wampool is common land; elsewhere, as at Allonby, Skinburness and Beckfoot, the County Council have acquired foreshore land as part of their policy of protection.

The sites of forts at Burgh and Bowness mark the western end of the Roman Wall, though there is little of it to see now; stones from the wall are part of the fabric of the church and other buildings at Bowness. Farther down the coast there were smaller Roman forts at Beckfoot and Maryport. Just south of Moricambe Bay, where the Waver and the Wampool reach the sea, were the lands of an important monastery, Holme Cultram Abbey, founded by King David of Scotland in the twelfth century. The remains now form part of the parish church at Abbey Town. The Solway area also has an exceptionally interesting transport history. Not only are there the Solway fords across Bow-ness and Dornock Waths used as short cuts from Dumfries by the more adventurous of the Scottish cattle drovers, but there are the remnants of the Solway viaduct just to the west and of the old Carlisle canal to the east. The latter had a short life, for the canal was soon drained and its bed ignomini-ously used as track for the railway, whose development had put the canal out of business. With the closure of the Carlisle to Silloth railway in 1964, the whole of the old link between Carlisle and its port has now gone.

The Solway Firth is also of great interest to the naturalist. There are a num-

Wide sands, wide skies and wide views at Bowness-on-Solway.

ber of Sites of Special Scientific Interest in the designated area, affording extra protection to the wildlife, which is of international significance; for this is one of the finest sites in Europe for flightings of wild ducks and geese, known alike to keen wildfowlers and ornithologists.

CENTRES   Carlisle, Maryport, Silloth

PLACES OF INTEREST   Abbey Town (Holme Cultram Abbey), Bowness-on-Solway, Burgh Marsh, Crosscanonby, Mawbray Bank, Rockcliffe Marsh, Skinburness

South Devon

Like North Devon a designation made in 1959 and confirmed in 1960, the South Devon area of 128 square miles stretches from Tor Bay to the outskirts of Plymouth and includes much of the region known as 'the South Hams'. It is an area of fine cliff scenery and long winding estuaries, so that it is difficult to see the whole without long detours; east-west progress is halted by the drowned valleys of the Dart, Avon, Earme and Yealm and by the Kingsbridge Estuary, which split the area into a number of largely isolated parts.

The diverse character of the rocks of the area can be seen in the varied and colourful cliff scenery, but again, as in many western coastal areas, little can be seen of this diversity from the appearance of the low coastal plateau, deeply dissected by its river valleys. This is because an earlier sea had planed off the surface of the land; at 200 feet above present sea level part of this wave-cut platform can be clearly seen near Brixham. Now the sea is working away again at the cliffs, while a rise in sea level in New Stone Age times drowned the lower part of the Dart and other valleys. Drowned forests too can be seen in Tor Bay. At Start Point, and between Bolt Head and Bolt Tail, the most colourful cliffs on this coast are carved from old Pre-Cambrian rocks similar to those of the Lizard.

From the eastern end of the area, which encloses the port of Brixham and includes the country park of Berry Head, the first main extension inland is along the Dart, almost as far as Totnes. This is an estuary that may be crossed by ferry, from Kingswear to Dartmouth, a crossing guarded by fifteenth-century Dartmouth Castle, which was re-armed for coastal defence as recently as 1940. Dartmouth has the handsome appearance of a prosperous port; when Defoe visited it he was lucky enough to see a shoal of pilchard come in and afterwards bought seventeen for a halfpenny. Winding on down the coast towards Start Point, the coast road passes along the spectacular raised beach of Slapton Sands, where, for over two miles, there is on one side the sea and on the other a mere which forms a refuge for wildfowl. There is a Field Studies Council nature reserve and centre at Slapton Ley.

Between the rugged cliffs of Start Point and Bolt Head another beautiful estuary winds inland, this time to Salcombe, a natural harbour and popular resort, and to Kingsbridge, which is just on the edge of the designated area. Besides the coast path that runs right through the area (see p. 237), there are many fine walks along the cliffs as far as Bolt Tail; much of the cliff-top land has been acquired by the National Trust.

Blackpool Sands near Dartmouth, and the coastline of Start Bay.

Near to the mouth of the Avon lies the resort of Bigbury-on-Sea with its curious 'sea trams' that go out to Burgh Island, just off-shore. Past the secret estuaries of the Erme and the Yealm, the three-mile-wide band of designated land gradually narrows to end at Dunstone Point on Plymouth Sound.

CENTRES   Brixham, Dartmouth, Paignton, Plymouth, Salcombe, Totnes

PLACES OF INTEREST   Berry Head Country Park, Bolt Head, Dartmouth Castle, Overbecks (gardens and museum), Salcombe Castle, Slapton Sands

195

South Hampshire Coast

Passengers on the ocean liners going into Southampton Water see on the port bow a low spit of land at the entrance to the estuary, and beyond it the vast complex of Fawley Refinery. Calshot Castle, the fort which occupies this spit, is the eastern limit of the South Hampshire Coast designated area; Hurst Castle, facing across to the Needles, is the western. The fourteen-mile

Buckler's Hard and the Beaulieu River.

strip of coast bordering the Solent is the basis of this area of thirty square miles, designated in 1967, but the central part extends inland up the Beaulieu River for about six miles and is bounded by the heathlands of the New Forest.

Between Calshot and the mouth of the Lymington River much of the coast has woods of oak and pine stretching down almost to the beach. At the western end, around Keyhaven and Lymington, there are some attractive examples of saltmarsh, a reminder of Lymington's once-flourishing salt trade. Hurst Castle, now under the care of the Department of the Environment, was first built in the reign of Henry VIII, and later became the last prison of Charles I before his execution. Clarendon records that the castle was situated 'in so vile and unwholesome an air that the common guards there used to be frequently changed for the preservation of their health', but nowadays it will be found much improved.

Beaulieu River, like Southampton Water, is part of a 'drowned' river system. In post-glacial times the sea level rose to breach the defences of the land and invade the low-lying Hampshire basin via the twin channels of the Solent and Spithead. It is this that gives the broad and beautiful stretches of water as far upstream as Beaulieu. In the seventeenth century the river was used for larger vessels than nowadays, and there was a busy shipyard at Buckler's Hard, only three miles down from Beaulieu.

Buckler's Hard and the right bank of the river are part of the Beaulieu Estate, which has many interests for visitors to the area. There is a maritime museum recording the shipbuilding days of the Hard, and the whole village street has been restored to much of its original appearance. At Beaulieu itself there are the Abbey, a Cistercian foundation dating back to the beginning of the thirteenth century, and Palace House, formerly the gate house of the Abbey but converted during the sixteenth century into a manor house. In addition there is the famous National Motor Museum. But the Estate also caters for specialist interests; near to the mouth of the river at Needs Ore Point is a fine bird sanctuary.

CENTRES   Beaulieu, Hythe, Lymington

PLACES OF INTEREST   Beaulieu, Buckler's Hard, Calshot Beach, Hurst Castle, Lepe

Suffolk Coast and Heaths

The coastline of Suffolk is the largest reserve of unspoiled coastline near to London. It has beautiful and unique features which have remained unspoilt largely because it is difficult to reach except in the north, its remoteness and inaccessibility stemming from the presence of the broad creeks and estuaries of the Blyth, Alde, Butley, Deben, Orwell and Stour rivers which have pushed the lines of communication inland. In 1969 a stretch of thirty-eight miles of this coastline, from Kessingland just south of Lowestoft to the Orwell opposite Harwich, was included in a 150-square-mile designated area of outstanding natural beauty. The area extends inland up to nearly eight miles in the Woodbridge and Rendlesham Forest regions, covers both banks of the Orwell almost to Ipswich and the north bank of the Stour almost to Brantham. The coast towns of Southwold and Aldeburgh lie within the area but most of Felixstowe is omitted.

From Kessingland to Aldeburgh the shore consists of alternating short stretches of cliffs and low-lying land, at one time inlets or river mouths. South of Aldeburgh is Orford Ness, the largest shingle spit on the east coast, where the River Alde, having got to within yards of the sea, is deflected south for eleven miles parallel to the coast. Orford, at one time a port of some substance, as shown by its strong castle, has been left some miles up river as the spit has progressed southwards. South of Orfordness at Bawdsey are some low cliffs of Red Crag, a relatively young deposit laid down just before the Ice Age. Though the shingle is building up protective banks in these southern stretches, farther north the coast is still receding. At Dunwich Cliffs you are supposed to be able to hear the ghostly bells of the long-drowned church, once part of a thriving mediaeval town.

The long estuaries of this coastline were formed when the land sank following the Ice Age and the sea was able to invade the river mouths. The upper reaches are often attractively wooded, and the Orwell, Deben and Alde are all popular for sailing. The town of Ipswich was granted the bed and foreshore of the Orwell in its Charter from Henry VIII in 1518, and has granted licences for the boating facilities at Woolverstone and Pin Mill.

The area is noted for the variety of wildlife and has special importance to ornithologists as one of the remaining homes of the graceful avocet. There are bird sanctuaries at Minsmere and Havergate Island (behind Orfordness) which is a national nature reserve, as are Westleton Heath, a survival of the once extensive heathlands, and Walberswick Reserve, which has heathland,

Orford Ness, the largest shingle spit on the east coast.

marsh and woods. Among the many attractive towns and villages in the area, Aldeburgh is well known for its music festival and its ancient Moot Hall, and Southwold has a fine church, notable for its patterned flintwork exterior.

CENTRES   Aldeburgh, Felixstowe, Ipswich, Southwold, Woodbridge

PLACES OF INTEREST   Aldeburgh, Benacre Broad, Blythburgh, Dunwich, Kyson Hill, Minsmere, Orford Castle, Orfordness, Snape (The Maltings), Southwold (museum), Sutton Hoo, Westleton Heath

199

Surrey Hills

The brick suburbs of London have long since spread out into the chalk country of the North Downs, but here they are softened by the shape of the land. The steep valleys and combes of the chalk dip-slope divide housing development into pockets even more successfully than the Green Belt woodlands. But the best scenery of the North Downs lies along the south-facing *cuesta,* as the geographer calls a hill ridge with a steep face on one side and a gentle slope on the other, and it is this that forms the spine of the Surrey Hills designated area.

This area of 160 square miles includes the Hog's Back from Farnham to Guildford, the Downs as far as Titsey Hill on the Kentish border, and the parallel ridge of the greensand to the south from Holmwood and Leith Hill back to Hindhead and the Hampshire county boundary. It is narrowly divided by the Wey Gap just south of Guildford, but meets up with the Sussex Downs area near Haslemere and with the North Kent Downs near

Fishing in the River Mole below the slopes of the North Downs near Mickleham.

Westerham. The designation, made in September 1956, was confirmed in May 1958.

The North Downs are both steeper and more wooded than the South Downs, and their height varies from nearly 900 feet at Botley Hill in the east of the area to less than 500 feet at the Hog's Back, where the chalk is dipping steeply into the ground, producing an almost symmetrical ridge. The greensand scarp at Leith Hill has a hard chert capping which has resisted erosion, so that at 965 feet this is the highest spot in south-east England. Farther west towards the Hampshire border the greensand supports what Cobbett called 'rascally heaths'; never one to mince words about unproductive land, he considered the area around Hindhead 'certainly the most villainous spot that God ever made'. Nowadays Frensham Common, Gibbet Hill and the Devil's Punchbowl are amongst the attractive properties of the National Trust in the area.

The slope of the Downs provided the open ground for one of the best-known trackways of the south-east—the Pilgrim's Way, which runs right through the area from Farnham to the foot of Titsey Hill. Parallel, but usually on the crest of the Downs, runs the North Downs Way (see p. 213). There are many fine villages worth visiting, such as Abinger, Chiddingfold, Hambledon, Shere and Thursley, as well as the Elizabethan manor of Loseley House, near Guildford, Polesden Lacey with its fine grounds and collections of pictures and furniture, and the Arboretum at Winkworth.

For some years now Surrey County Council have pursued a policy of buying land along the line of the Downs as Public Open Spaces. These, together with National Trust land at such popular places as Box Hill, Leith Hill and Ranmore Common, have ensured that there is good public access throughout much of the area. Some parts are indeed over-used, because of their proximity to London, but as more country parks are established the present pressures will probably be eased. More vigorous management and wardening at Box Hill and Burford Bridge is already improving these well-visited spots.

CENTRES   Dorking, Farnham, Guildford, Haslemere, Red-hill, Reigate, Westerham

PLACES OF INTEREST   Box Hill, Frensham Common, Gatton Park, Hindhead (Devil's Punch Bowl), Leith Hill, Loseley Manor, Norbury Park, Polesden Lacey, Ranmore Common, Shere, Winkworth Arboretum

Sussex Downs

Take any of the roads from London to the South Coast, from the A3 Portsmouth Road to the A22 Eastbourne Road, and the pattern of the countryside is very similar. One crosses the chalk and greensand hills of Surrey, and then the still well-wooded area of the Weald. Beyond this a long line of characteristic chalk hills appears ahead, smooth and rounded in outline. These are the South Downs, stretching from Hampshire eastwards towards the Channel, with the line of resorts from Bognor to Brighton tucked in behind them.

The South Downs, with the Norfolk Broads, were included among the twelve national parks proposed in the Hobhouse Report of 1947. It was not until 1956 that they were dropped from the list, when the National Parks Commission decided that this form of designation was not appropriate; their surveys had shown that the recreational value of the Downs had been eroded by extensive cultivation. It is certain that there were fewer fences on the Downs before the last war, less land under the plough, more sheep, and a tendency to find dewponds rather than water tanks on the heights. But the Commission were well aware that there was still very much that needed some form of protection, and they pressed ahead with the designation of 379 square miles of the Downs in Sussex, including nearly all the chalk lands and greensand hills, plus land across the Rother Valley and north to Blackdown, where the area adjoins the Surrey Hills (see p. 200). Designation of this large and complex area was not easy, but eventually, after many delays, the order was made in 1965 and confirmed in 1966.

The scarp of the Downs is broken by four river gaps—the Arun, Adur, Ouse and Cuckmere valleys. But on the dip slope there are many of the characteristic dry valleys of the chalk, left by rivers that have disappeared underground. Where the Downs are cut across in section by the sea, between Seaford and Eastbourne, it is these valleys that form the Seven Sisters. This short stretch of coastline is one of the finest in the country, culminating in the 500-foot dizzying cliffs of Beachy Head. From the northern edge of the Downs there are fine views over the Weald for walkers or riders on the South Downs Way (see p. 230), which follows the length of the designated area from Eastbourne to the Hampshire border.

The area is richer in history than in natural history. Evidence of man's activity goes back to the ancient earthworks, grazing grounds, field systems, tumuli, barrows and flint mines. But nearer to the present day, Defoe noted that Arun mullet were accounted the largest in England, and that wheatears,

The scarp of the Downs at Windover Hill, and the Long Man of Wilmington.

then a delicacy, were cheaper on the Downs than at Tunbridge. Besides the downland villages, worth days of exploring, there are fine houses and park/ land to visit at Uppark on the western, Petworth and Parham on the nor/ thern, boundaries of the area, luncheon or tea at Goodwood House (by appointment), where there is also a country park, Glyndebourne for opera, and Glynde Place, a sixteenth/century manor in the native flint and brick. Near Singleton lies the Weald and Downland open/air Museum, with demonstrations of the building, crafts and industry of the area.

CENTRES   Brighton, Chichester, Eastbourne, Hove, Lewes, Petersfield, Worthing

PLACES OF INTEREST   Alfriston, Arundel Castle, Beachy Head, Bignor (Roman villa), Bramber (St Mary's, castle), Chanctonbury Ring, Charleston Manor (near Westdean), Cissbury Ring, Devil's Dyke, Ditchling Beacon, Eastdean, Firle Place, Glynde/ bourne, Glynde Place, Goodwood Park and House, Kingley Vale, Parham House, Petworth House, Seven Sisters, Steyning, Uppark, Weald and Downland Open/Air Museum, Wilmington (Long Man)

203

The famous view over the Wye from Symonds Yat Rock.

Wye Valley

The Wye Valley has long been famous for its beauty. In 1770 that expert on the subject of picturesque beauty, William Gilpin, made a journey through the area, on which he later published his Observations. Not very much later, in 1798, Wordsworth visited the Wye Valley on a walking tour with his sister, composing the famous lines on the banks of the river a few miles above Tintern Abbey. 'No poem of mine', he wrote, 'was composed under circumstances more pleasant for me than this.' It was appropriate, therefore, that plans to designate some 124 miles of the Wye Valley were announced in 1970, the bicentenary year of the poet's birth, as well as of Gilpin's visit.

The designated area extends from Chepstow to within three miles of Hereford. It varies from $2\frac{1}{2}$ to 5 miles in width, encompassing the broad meanders of the river above Ross in the north, and in the south including Chepstow Park Wood and the pleasant hilly country along the back road from Chepstow to Monmouth through Trelech, from which there are fine views across to the Black Mountains. Such well-known places as Tintern Abbey and Symond's Yat lie within its boundaries. So does the town of Ross, compact and clustering around 'that heaven-directed spire'. The Man of Ross celebrated by Pope in his *Essay on Man* was John Kyrle, a public benefactor who built the town a causeway and raised the church spire 100 feet.

Below Ross the Wye Valley is characterised by steep slopes, cliffs and gorges. Its winding course is, however, that of a mature river, and it is clear that a gradual raising of the land surface has forced the river to deepen its bed without giving it time to widen the valley again except in one or two places such as Redbrook and Bigsweir where the cliffs marking the river's former course stand back from its newer, straighter, line. The graceful horseshoe bend that can be seen from Symonds Yat is famous, but the slightly smaller example just above Chepstow where the river bends under the precipitous Wyndcliff is not to be missed. The limestone cliffs are here, and in many other places, quite well wooded, and the Wyndcliff is a Forest Nature Reserve with a rich flora. Wintour's Leap (the leap must surely be legendary) offers another fine viewpoint, a little farther downstream, over the Wye's winding course.

At Chepstow the area includes the magnificent ruins of the Castle, which stands on a cliff above the river, defended on the other side by a deep dell which provides a pleasant open space for the town. Another fine castle within the area is that at Goodrich, its rich red sandstone a sharp contrast with the grey limestone of Chepstow. Gilpin, resting on his oars, thought the view one of the grandest on the river though not 'correctly picturesque'.

CENTRES	Chepstow, Hereford, Monmouth, Ross-on-Wye
PLACES OF INTEREST	Chepstow Castle, Goodrich Castle, The Kymin (near Monmouth), St Briavel's Castle, Symonds Yat, Tintern Abbey, Trelech, Wintour's Leap, Wyndcliff

3

LONG-DISTANCE FOOTPATHS
AND BRIDLEWAYS

Continuous rights of way over some of the country's finest mountain, moor-land, downland and coastal scenery were recommended by the other Hob-house Committee (see p. 22) on Footpaths and Access to the Countryside, and provision was made in the National Parks Act of 1949 for bringing these into being. The Committee had suggested the Pennine Way, a Pil-grims' Way running from Winchester to Canterbury, a Thames towpath walk from Cricklade to Teddington, a South Downs walk, and a walk of some 260 miles from the Gog Magog Hills in Cambridgeshire, along the Chil-terns and over the Marlborough Downs and the Dorset downland to finish at Seaton Bay in Devon. On these paths, which were to avoid roads used by vehicles as far as possible, people would be able to make long journeys on foot or on horseback. The routes were to be chosen for their scenic qualities rather than as a means of getting from one place to another or a mere linking of existing rights of way.

By 1951 the National Parks Commission had submitted recommenda-tions for the Pennine Way, the proposed route had been approved, and the Minister expressed the hope that the local authorities, whose job it was to secure the creation of the new rights of way over ninety-one miles for which no rights existed, would have completed their work by 1st April 1952, so that the whole route could be available by Easter. The first of April came and went fourteen times before the Pennine Way was officially opened, which illus-trates some of the difficulties that the making of these paths presented. For the local authorities, often small and inadequately equipped councils in remote areas, the first task of ascertaining ownership was often the stumbling block; then came tedious negotiations, matters of compensation, and in some cases compulsory orders.

Progress towards the completion of the national long-distance footpaths and bridleways so far submitted by the National Parks and Countryside Com-missions and approved by Ministers has speeded up today, thanks to a task force of officers at the Countryside Commission who were able to assist local authorities in their work of negotiation. Since the Cleveland Way opened in

1969, new long-distance footpaths and bridleways have been opening at the rate of one a year.

It was at no time intended that these paths should be paths in any formal sense, built and surfaced by highway authorities. Often they traverse rough country and are hard going even for experienced walkers. Ability to use a map and compass is necessary on the Pennine Way and parts of the Cleveland Way, while the coast paths, though presenting fewer problems of navigation, have other hazards like high winds on exposed cliff-tops, wet and slippery surfaces, and coast erosion. Waymarking is carried out, using the Countryside Commission's acorn waymark sign, but only as an occasional guide; walkers and riders are expected to carry maps or the official guidebook where it is available. On the Pennine Way mapboards have been sited at intervals along the way, but they are intended mostly as a check for those carrying unmarked maps and as a means of drawing attention to the Way. The Commission has produced leaflets describing many of the paths, official guidebooks are being published as soon as possible after the opening of each path, and the Ordnance Survey are including the line of the paths on new editions of their 1-inch and 1/50,000 maps.

A final word of warning is necessary for those planning walks along the Pembrokeshire and South West Coast paths, also the coastal sections of the Cleveland Way. Cliff climbing is for the specialist, and walkers should not be tempted to climb; neither should they allow themselves to be forced into cliff climbing by insufficient attention to the state of the tide. Particularly in the South West there are many creeks and estuaries to cross, and at some of these ferry services are uncertain or non-existent at certain times of year. The best plan is to enquire locally about the best means of crossing, and preferably do this beforehand, as sometimes a long detour may be necessary.

Some of the paths, again particularly the coast paths, can be appreciated in short stretches, between resorts for instance. On others, footpaths giving access to the long-distance path may enable one to make a circuit taking in one of its finest viewpoints—for most of the paths are picked for the views they give. To some the whole path will present a challenge and enable one to finish a holiday spent on it with a sense of achievement. And to many who will probably never walk even a short stretch of a long-distance path their existence is an inspiration: it is splendid just to know that one could.

Cleveland Way

From Helmsley to Filey by road is some thirty-six miles, an hour's drive along the length of the level Vale of Pickering. By the Cleveland Way it could take ten days or more of walking, one hundred miles of moorland and cliff top in a gigantic arc, but I think that few could complete the journey without acquiring a taste for this fascinating part of Yorkshire.

The Cleveland Way clings to the edge of the vast block of the North Yorkshire Moors, one of the largest expanses of heather moor in the country. Cleveland is 'cliff-land' and whether you are on the coastal or inland stretches of the Way, the appropriateness of the name is obvious. On the one hand there is either the sea or the plain, on the other the high ground of the moors. But the Way did not always have this name. It was first drawn up under the cumbersome title of 'North York Moors and Coast Path', and it was not until less than a year before the official opening took place on a showery May day at Helmsley Castle that the present name, urged by local users of the Way, was substituted.

Not far from the church in Helmsley, the Cleveland Way leaves the town by a well-defined path off the Bilsdale and Stokesley road. On the left is the tall ruined keep of Helmsley Castle and beyond is Duncombe Park, which the path skirts for a while before emerging onto the terrace of Whinny Bank above the River Rye. At the narrow, hump-backed Rievaulx bridge the Way crosses the river, less than half a mile from the magnificent ruins of Rievaulx Abbey with its beautiful position 'among a Brotherhood of valleys', as Dorothy Wordsworth described it. William and Dorothy, those grand walkers, reached the Abbey on the evening of a hot July day, having set out from Thirsk where, to the rude amusement of the landlady at the Three Tuns, they had left their post-chaise that morning.

Threading its way through wooded valleys branching to left and right, the path emerges on to the limestone uplands at the village of Cold Kirby. Past Hambleton House, an old-established racing stables with some fine gallops over the surrounding 900-foot plateau, you reach the first really steep cliff on the Way at Sutton Bank, and can overlook the broad Vale of York to the Pennines beyond. To take advantage of the fine views there is small detour southwards here, along the scarp edge, which makes a famous site for gliding, to the White Horse of Kilburn. This 300-foot figure cut into the bank is of nineteenth-century origin, unlike some of its relatives in the south, and, lacking the whiteness of the chalkland horses, actually has to be white-washed.

Looking along the Cleveland escarpment from Cringle Moor. After following the line of summits eastward the Way strikes north along the top of Greenhow Bank, seen in the background.

These first nine miles or so of the Way have taken you from east to west; now the line is northwards along an ancient route taken by the drovers who brought cattle from Scotland and Northumberland. Before joining the drove road proper, though, there is another fine cliff-edge walk above Gormire Lake and along Boltby Scar to Sneck Yat (gate), where a road back into Ryedale crosses the scarp. From High Paradise the path follows the old drove road for some seven miles, climbing to over 1200 feet and skirting the massive hill of Black Hambleton. Droving started to decline half-way through the last century, when railways began to carry livestock in greater numbers, but the high Hambleton road, avoiding costly turnpikes, must have had a fair traffic flow: there are the remains of at least one inn along the Way. Cattle were temporarily shod for their journey, and even geese, which also travelled this way, were given a tarmacadam tread by driving them first through wet tar and grit. The road goes straight on northwards towards the Cleveland scarp and the River Tees at Yarm, but the Cleveland Way breaks off down Oakdale, with its two small reservoirs, to emerge at length by a small lane into the centre of Osmotherley.

Only a short way north of Osmotherley, the Cleveland Way, now really in Cleveland, turns eastwards along the line of promontories that make up the scarp of the Cleveland Hills. From Scarth Nick, where you meet once again, and this time cross, the old drove road, you are also more likely to meet fellow walkers. For some twelve miles the Cleveland Way follows the same path as the notorious Lyke Wake Walk, a forty-mile, twenty-four-hour endurance test straight across the watershed of the moors to Ravenscar on the coast, undertaken by thousands every year. Our path will also go to Ravenscar, but by a longer and more rewarding route, with the prizes for those that can pause oftenest. And there is plenty to pause for over this part of the Way as well; the path switchbacks over Carlton Bank, Cringle Moor, Cold Moor and Hasty Bank, with fine views in either direction along the scarp and out over the plain. On Urra Moor the Way climbs to its highest point—and indeed the highest point on the Moors—at Botton Head, nearly 1500 feet above sea level. Bleak though the moors appear, they were crossed by many historic tracks: near Botton Head and beyond are a number of stone signposts, as well as carved boundary marker stones.

At the point where the old ironstone railway, closed in the 1920s, comes snaking across the moors from Rosedale, the Cleveland Way bends northwards again following the top of Greenhow Bank to Kildale. It then climbs Easby Moor, where a sturdy monument to Captain Cook stands. Cook went to school in Great Ayton, where there is now a small museum recording this association. From Ayton Moor there is a small detour westwards to climb Roseberry Topping, a craggy hill that has been in view for many miles of the way along the Cleveland Hills, but the path then strikes out for the coast, past Highcliff, another fine viewpoint, Guisborough and Skelton and the old mining district of Cleveland to reach the sea at Saltburn.

From now on the Cleveland Way is a coast path. The first big cliff out of Saltburn is Hunt Cliff, on which stand the remains, still just visible, of a Roman signal station. There follows a sharp reminder of the Cleveland iron industry; Skinningrove contains in its narrow valley the mines, furnaces, and slag tips and terrace houses that sum up that busy nineteenth century development. But the next headland soon hides it, and you are now on the massive bulk of Boulby Cliff, the highest on the coasts of England. This too has been scarred in the past by quarrying, chiefly for the alum industry, and now has below it the concrete structures of Britain's first potash mine, but even this does nothing to dent its grandeur. Looking back towards the cliff on the way down to Staithes, you may, at certain times, see the drifting of smoke with a more natural origin, the spontaneous combustion of the alum shales.

Staithes is still a working port and lobster fishery and the old part preserves its attractive untidiness, all cramped cottages and precipitous alleyways. The elaborate Staithes bonnets may sometimes be seen, if not worn then drying on lines in the tiny yards. Past the deserted harbour of Port Mulgrave, the path reaches Runswick Bay, first of the fine bays on this coast, its old fishing village now given over to holiday visitors. The southern limit of the bay is the headland of Kettleness, with its gigantic alum excavations, and beyond this the path emerges onto Lythe Bank and a fine view of Whitby.

Whitby stands on the mouth of the Esk (a little nameless river, indeed scarce worth a name, commented Defoe), which is guarded by the West and East Cliffs. The Way climbs out of the old part of the town up the 199 steps to the grotesque old sea-going parish church and the extraordinary ruins of Whitby Abbey defying on-shore and off-shore winds in a bleak site better suited to a light-house. The light-house stands, in fact, a little farther down the coast, and when the cliffs are clothed in the clinging 'roke' or North Sea mist one may hear the roar of the 'Whitby Bull' foghorn every ninety seconds. A further fine stretch of cliff path now leads to the North Cheek of Robin Hood's Bay, which sweeps round to the lofty cliff of Ravenscar, some 600 feet up from the beach. Along the top of Beast Cliff to the wooded, boulder-strewn inlets of Hayburn Wyke and Cloughton Wyke, the Cleveland Way follows the coast to Scarborough's North Bay. It then re-starts at the other end of South Bay, and continues past Cornelian and Cayton Bays as far as the county boundary with the East Riding less than two miles short of Filey.

The Cleveland Way crams an immense variety of scene into its hundred miles. In fine weather it is a walk for everyone, but the moorland stretches can also be a test for the toughest. Along the coastal section there has been much erosion of the boulder-clay cliffs and reasonable care is needed on cliff-edge paths.

North Downs Way

The eleventh long-distance footpath to be approved, the North Downs Way, covers 141 miles from Farnham in Surrey to Dover in Kent and follows, wherever possible, the crest of the North Downs. It coincides in only a few places with the mediaeval Pilgrims' Way from Winchester to Canterbury, much of which has now become a busy road unsuitable for long-distance walkers. But in any case the North Downs Way is primarily a scenic path, chosen to follow a physical rather than a historical feature. The pilgrims preferred to keep to a middle line, above the forests of the clay vale but below the exposed hilltops. Their eyes fixed on the Way to Canterbury, they were less than interested in views of the Weald.

The path starts near Farnham railway station on the A31 road. For a short distance it follows the River Wey, before crossing it and reaching higher ground just north of Crooksbury Hill. Passing close by the village of Seale, it keeps just south of the Hog's Back, the crest of which is occupied by the A31 road, and, crossing the north end of Puttenham Common, goes through Puttenham village. The path passes under the Guildford By-pass and skirting the north side of Loseley Park reaches the River Wey Navigation just south of Guildford. A ferry operated here for the pilgrims, whose Way now coincides with the long-distance path, but a footbridge at St Catherine's is proposed for the new crossing. The reputed Pilgrims' Way is certainly a historic trackway and its line is now followed over St Martha's Hill and along Albury Downs from Newlands Corner to Netley Heath. Here it is on the line of the chalk escarpment, rising to over 700 feet at Netley Heath and giving extensive views southward. This was also a route followed by drovers from as far west as Wales on their way to markets like that at Maidstone in Kent.

Continuing over White Downs and Ranmore Common it burrows under the busy A24 road north of Dorking to reach the Mole at the foot of Box Hill. The crossing here is either by the famous stepping stones or by the footbridge a little way downstream. Climbing Box Hill, the path follows the escarpment, well above the line of the Pilgrims' Way, past Betchworth and Buckland Hills, Colley and Reigate Hills, to cross the Reigate road by a footbridge. It keeps below the hill crest road on Wingate Hill and skirts the north side of Gatton Park to Merstham, where about 300 yards of the A23 Brighton Road must be followed northwards before the path starts off east again to White Hill and Gravelly Hill. The A22 Eastbourne Road is the next main obstacle and here a footbridge has been proposed. The stretch immediately

The view westwards along the Downs from Colley Hill, above Reigate.

beyond descends from the crest of the Downs, which is again occupied by a road, to avoid extensive quarrying operations. But it is still high enough to give good views to the south.

At Tatsfield the path enters Kent. It follows the slopes of the downs as far as Chevening Park, which is crossed by a diagonal path, and continues through Dunton Green and across the Darent Valley to Otford, where it again joins the Pilgrims' Way. Past the Roman Villa site at Otford, the path climbs to the top of the downs again and keeps to the wooded scarp. At Wrotham there is no special crossing over the busy A20, but this is best done at the roundabout above Wrotham village, and the path then runs almost parallel to the Meopham road for two miles.

Just north of Trottiscliffe the path sets out again along the escarpment by Whitehorse Wood and Holly Hill until it emerges above the Medway just upriver from Rochester. The Medway is crossed by the footbridge that runs alongside the M2 motorway, and the path then curves south again by Bluebell Hill to Detling. It continues parallel to the Pilgrims' Way but upslope, past Thurnham Castle and Cat Mount to Hollingbourne, where both Ways coincide again. They run together to Charing and then drop gradually through orchard country to Wye.

At Boughton Aluph, just before Wye, the Canterbury loop alternative branches off to the north-east past Soakham Down and around Godmersham and Chilham Park to enter Chilham village. From there it passes mainly through orchard lands to reach Canterbury at Harbledown. East of the city it leaves the Roman road to Sandwich and strikes south-east, again through orchards, to Patrixbourne. Over Barham Downs it runs parallel to the Dover Road for three miles before bending east through Waldershare Park to join the Roman road running due south into Dover.

The main route passes through Wye and, climbing the downs again near Hastingleigh, runs through Stowting and past Etchinghill to Cherry Garden, Castle, and Sugarloaf Hills just north of Folkestone. After crossing the main road into Folkestone just by Sugarloaf Hill, the path follows Creteway Downs to reach the town end of Folkestone Warren at the Valiant Sailor public house. From here there is a cliff-top path to Dover, but when firing ranges at Lydden Spout are in action a detour along the coast road is necessary. The path finishes at Shakespeare Cliff, overlooking the port.

Though some miles of rights of way remain to be cleared on the North Downs Way, a section of forty-three miles, including the Canterbury Loop, was declared open by Kent County Council in 1972.

Offa's Dyke Path

'Long-distance routes will be based upon some strong physical or historic feature', said the National Parks Commission in their second annual report, in which they also listed Offa's Dyke as a route being surveyed. There could hardly be a stronger physical and historic feature than the great earth-work built by Offa, the powerful eighth-century King of Mercia, as a boundary line between his kingdom and the lands of the Welsh. The dyke is still an impressive feature along many stretches of the path as it snakes over the hills of the Welsh Marches, though in two stretches, one in the north and one in the south, where few indications of its line remain, the path seizes the opportunity to climb over high moorland areas. It seems likely that the dyke was never considered as a line of defence, but rather in the same way as a modern ploughed-strip inland frontier between nations. As a negotiated frontier it was subject to laws governing those who crossed it from either side, particularly those who crossed it with stolen cattle.

The path's southern end is marked by a stone on the cliffs of the Severn estuary at Sedbury, in full view of the great span of the Severn Bridge. From here it makes for Chepstow, passing the ends of the two Wye bridges, Brunel's spectacular tube structure and the road bridge with its impressive background of Chepstow Castle, but keeps to the Gloucestershire bank. Climbing Tutshill, it follows in part the narrow Donkey Lane to Wintour's Leap, a spectacular cliff viewpoint beneath which the Wye makes a great U-bend. The banks of the Wye are well-wooded all along the next stretch to Shorn Cliff and the Devil's Pulpit, and it is in these woods that the dyke makes its appearance as an impressive earth bank. There are fine views of Tintern Abbey in the valley below. There are alternative routes just beyond here, following either the line of the dyke as it crosses St Briavel's Common or the line of the river from Brockweir to Bigsweir.

The path continues to keep close to the Wye until, just east of Monmouth, it climbs the hill and viewpoint of the Kymin, topped by a small memorial temple dedicated to naval heroes. On the way it passes two small areas of former industry, reminders of the nearby Forest of Dean. Gilpin, in 1770, found the wharf at Lydbrook most pleasing: 'the engines used in lading and unlading, together with the solemnity of the scene, produce all together a picturesque assemblage'. Descending into the town of Monmouth, the path crosses the Wye and Monnow, the latter by the famous fortified gatehouse

Chepstow Castle seen across the Wye from the Gloucestershire bank, which is followed by the Path.

bridge, and strikes out across pleasant pastoral countryside towards one of the trio of impressive Border castles in the area, White Castle.

At Pandy, not far ahead, the path starts on the long climb to the eastern ridge of the Black Mountains. This is a fine moorland stretch, rising to over 2000 feet along a broad ridge with views to the left into the valley of the Honddu and to the right past Longtown to the Herefordshire plain. Hay Bluff marks the end of the sandstone 'darren' over which the path has passed, but the route down to Hay-on-Wye avoids the steep scarp face of the Black Mountains. There are fine views across the broad Wye valley to the rolling country of Radnorshire which the path is to cross.

From Hay to the valley of the Arrow and on to Gladestry, the path is in

the Kilvert Country. The diary of Francis Kilvert paints a fascinating picture of the life of the countryside in mid-Victorian times as seen by an impres-
sionable and susceptible young curate. Beyond Kington the dyke is again
much in evidence on Rushock and Herrock Hills and the path follows its
course, past a dyke marker stone on the Presteigne–Knighton road, and down
the Ffridd into Knighton. Here, in July 1971, the path was officially opened
by Lord Hunt; over two thousand people attended the ceremony at Pinner's
Hole, where the path goes down to the Teme, and a small park, containing a
section of the dyke, was dedicated to the town of Knighton (known in
Welsh as Tref-y-Clawdd—the town on the dyke). A two-ton boulder bears
plaques commemorating the occasion.

Across the Teme the path enters Shropshire, meeting the dyke again at
the top of Panpunton Hill and following it over a fine stretch on Llanvair
Hill and Spoad Hill before descending from the upland of Clun Forest into
the lowland area around Montgomery. A straight stretch of dyke takes the
path across the plain, and it then climbs the Long Mountain to the hill fort
of Beacon Ring, before dropping to cross the Severn at Buttington. The path
keeps to the banks of the river for a while, but then curves away through
Llanymynech and continues north, finding another good length of dyke at
Baker's Hill, west of Oswestry. Just beyond the River Ceiriog the path skirts
the park of Chirk Castle, a fourteenth-century border castle continuously inhabited for 650 years, and then climbs over into the valley of the Dee.

High above the Dee goes Telford's great Pontcysyllte Aqueduct carrying
the Llangollen Canal. The path goes along its towpath, a dizzying 120 feet
up, to follow the Vale of Llangollen westwards under the crags of Eglwyseg
Mountain. Below lies the town of Llangollen, famous for its international
eisteddfodau, and, nearer the path, the ruins of Dinas Bran are perched on a
steep hill. The path keeps close to the massive mountain limestone scar looking across the Eglwyseg Glen to the road that ascends the Horseshoe Pass.
Curving northwards the scarp is broken by the intake known as The End
of the World, where there are a number of abandoned lead mines. From here
the path strikes across the moors north-west to the village of Llandegla.

Beyond Llandegla the path crosses and re-crosses the River Alun before
entering its second high ridge walk section—along the Clwydian Hills.
Several of the summits of this range are crowned by hill forts, the largest of
them, Pen-y-Cloddiau, covering some fifty acres. On Moel Fammau (1820
feet) stands a tower commemorating the Jubilee of George III—in 1820.
Through Bodfari, with more disused mines, and over the foothills of the
Clwydian Hills, the path at last emerges onto a gorse-clad bluff overlooking
Prestatyn. Many will want to complete their walk of this last section by con-
tinuing through the resort to the beach and the sea.

Pembrokeshire Coast Path

Soon after the designation of the Pembrokeshire Coast National Park, the National Parks Commission submitted proposals for a long-distance footpath following the cliffs, bays and beaches of its fine coastline from the county boundary with Carmarthen right round to the Teifi estuary opposite Cardigan in the north. A survey of this path of 168 miles had already been made for the Commission by the author and naturalist, R. M. Lockley. Eventually, after the long years of negotiation for the rights of way needed to complete the line, the path was officially opened in 1970 at Saundersfoot by Wynford Vaughan Thomas, himself a keen walker and owner of a property on the path. It was the third national path to be opened and the first in Wales.

The path makes it easier for people to explore and enjoy the distinctive character of the national park, for much of the coastline and the magnificent seascapes can be appreciated only by walkers on the cliffs. But the path also opens up many miles of coast to increasing numbers of visitors and holiday-makers ready to leave their cars for an hour or so. As with most coast paths, there are few serious route-finding problems, and in any case an energetic programme of waymarking with wooden 'Coast Path' signs and with the acorn waymark, has been carried out by the national park warden service. In places the line of the path had to be prepared by using a small bulldozer and a great deal of skill and courage on steeply sloping cliffland. On little-used sections the most formidable problem is the rapid growth of buckthorn in the generous climate of Pembrokeshire, but a scheme for regular maintenance and a greater degree of use as the path becomes better known should together remove difficulties.

The Pembrokeshire Coast Path may be walked starting from Amroth in the south or from St Dogmaels in the north; here it is described from south to north, or clockwise round the peninsula of Pembrokeshire. At Amroth a submerged forest can be seen at low tide, evidence of the changing levels of the sea which have done so much to shape the country of Pembrokeshire through which the path is to pass. The path sets out westward around a wide sandy bay, over Wiseman's Bridge and past the grounds of Hean Castle to the sailing resort of Saundersfoot. It then rounds wooded Monkstone Point to drop down to Tenby's North Shore. With its colour-washed Regency houses and its mediaeval walled centre, Tenby is a delightful resort, though easily overcrowded in peak holiday times. The path resumes above the two-mile stretch of the South Beach and continues along the limestone cliffs from Giltar Point to Lydstep Haven. Offshore lies Caldey Island, with its monastery, which can be visited by boat from Tenby.

The path now makes its way by an inland detour to Manorbier, for while Lydstep Point is National Trust property, Old Castle Head is a Services training area. A further area at Penally may also involve a detour, unless a check has been made beforehand that no firing is to take place. In any case such areas should be avoided when the red warning flags are flying. The Norman castle at Manorbier, standing on the valley rim about half a mile from the beach, was the birthplace of the chronicler Giraldus Cambrensis. The path continues around the coast, past the little harbour of Stackpole Quay and the fine viewpoint of Stackpole Head, to Bosherston. On the other side of the deep valley penetrating inland there is another larger training area extending over to Castlemartin and Freshwater West and putting out of bounds a stretch of coast including St Govan's Head with its tiny chapel, the deep cleft of Huntsman's Leap, Elegug Stack, the Green Bridge of Wales and Linney Head. Access may be possible over part of this area but, again, must be checked beforehand; otherwise an inland detour from Bosherston village by road to Castlemartin must be followed.

At Freshwater West the path rejoins the coast, and continues round the Angle Peninsula and along the shores of Angle Bay to Pwllcrochan and on into Pembroke. It crosses Monkton Bridge, just beyond the great castle of Pembroke, birthplace of Henry Tudor, and makes its way through Pembroke Dock to the ferry at Hobbs Point across to Neyland. From here the path follows the northern shore of the Haven through the town of Milford Haven and across the wooded inlet of Sandy Haven to Dale Harbour. Through the little yachting port of Dale it goes out to the tip of the Dale Peninsula at St Ann's Head, a good viewpoint where one can also see a spectacular example of folded rocks in the inlet just beyond the lighthouse and coastguard station. A fine stretch of path follows, with the islands of Skokholm and Skomer in view, along Marloes Sands and past the small detached peninsula of Gateholm, to Wooltack Point. The path crosses the neck of the point just by the earthworks of the promontory fort and continues by the little inlet of St Brides Haven and the offshore Stack Rocks to the twin resorts of Little Haven and Broad Haven. Maps and advice are available at the Pembrokeshire Countryside Unit, a small building at the far end of the car park at Broad Haven.

The path leads on around St Brides Bay past the little fishing hamlet of Nolton Haven, along the pebble ridge that backs Newgale Sands, and over some National Trust land to the little harbour of Solva, an anchorage for fishing boats and pleasure craft. Beyond Solva there is more Trust land as the path continues above Caerbwdi and Caerfai Bays, from whose colourful

The Path following the edge of the inlet towards the little harbour of Solva.

cliffs the stone for St David's cathedral was quarried. Across Ramsey Sound lies the long outline of Ramsey Island and beyond it the menacing Bishop and Clerk Rocks as the path turns northwards towards Whitesand Bay and St David's Head. From here onwards the coastline becomes more rugged as it progresses into North Pembrokeshire past the beautiful bay of Abereiddy and the precipitous harbour of Porth Gain. Beyond Trevine it passes near to the impressive cromlech of Carreg Samson just before reaching the inlet of Abercastle, and then sets off along steeper and higher cliffs to Strumble Head, around the cove of Pwll Deri and under the 700-foot fort-crowned Garn Fawr.

At Carregwastad Point, just before Fishguard Bay, a tablet commemorates the last invasion of Britain in 1797, when a small force of French irregulars landed and set up camp only to be captured almost immediately by the local militia. Leaving the port of Fishguard by the steep road up from the delightful Lower Town, the path climbs over rugged cliffs to Dinas Island, where there is a loop out to Dinas Head or a route across the neck of the peninsula to Cwm-yr-eglwys. Past the resort of Newport, with its broad sands and commanding castle set on the higher ground that slopes up to Carn Ingli, is another fine cliff section, notably at Ceibwr Bay, before the path reaches Cemaes Head and turns inland along the estuary of the Teifi to finish at St Dogmaels, a fishing port facing across the river to Cardigan.

Pennine Way

The Pennine Way is the best-known of the long-distance footpaths, running for 250 miles from the Peak District of Derbyshire along the Pennines and over the Cheviots to the Scottish Border. Though the full distance remains a test even for seasoned walkers, the idea of a continuous path is an inspiring one, and to follow the path even just for a mile or two over the wide fell tops from one dale to the next can be an unforgettable experience. It was an idea proposed and fought for by Tom Stephenson, now President of the Ramblers' Association and still a walker more active than his years would suggest. First of the long-distance footpaths, the Way was opened at Malham Moor in 1965, where over two thousand people gathered for the open-air occasion.

The first stretch of the way over the vast plateaux of Kinder and Bleaklow is a daunting one, and has found out many inadequately trained and prepared walkers. In bad weather Kinder is no place to be, however well-prepared, and accordingly, from the start at Edale, there are alternative paths, one ascending the steep Grindsbrook to cross the plateau through the bewildering peat groughs, and the other skirting the edge of the plateau to Upper Booth and climbing by Jacob's Ladder and Edale Cross to follow its western edge. The two routes meet at Kinder Downfall, where the river tumbles over the steep gritstone edge, and the Way continues north-west to Mill Hill before striking out north-east past Ashop Head and over the moor to the Snake Pass road.

Just beyond the Snake road the Way crosses Doctor's Gate, an old Roman road. Throughout its length the Pennine Way follows many miles of old paths and bridleways, pack-horse and drove roads, shepherds' and miners' tracks, old Roman roads and green lanes. But here the Way sets out along Devil's Dike and onto the great expanse of Bleaklow, with more peat groughs which must be crossed before the path descends north-westward into Longdendale by Torside Clough. From here there is another climb to Black Hill, where again there are alternative routes, the westerly branch via Wessenden Head being preferable after wet weather to the inky peat of the summit.

At the narrow neck of the Pennines crossed by the A62 the Way sets out along Standedge to Windy Hill where the new M62 motorway is spanned by an elegant footbridge. Another more spectacular gritstone edge follows—Blackstone, quaintly termed by Defoe 'the Andes of England'. Over the Calder Valley and round the head of Hebden Water, the Way reaches the moors of the Brontë country west of Haworth, and then by Cowling, Lothersdale and the viewpoint of Pinhaw Beacon descends into the lowland country of Craven.

For one mile, just north of Thornton-in-Craven, the Pennine Way becomes surprisingly a canal towpath, where the Leeds and Liverpool threads its way from Airedale across the Pennines. Then, meeting the Aire at Gargrave, the Way enters the Yorkshire Dales National Park, and runs across the moors parallel to Airedale, rejoining the river at the village of Airton. The head of Airedale is often known as Malhamdale. Just south of Malham the river springs from the ground, having followed an underground course from the limestone plateau above Malham Cove. Passing through Malham the Way climbs round the western side of this impressive cliff and sets out across the limestone pavements and past Malham Tarn. On Fountains Fell, just beyond, the old shafts of mines can be seen near the summit and a track beyond going down into the valley.

Ahead now lies the splendid profile of Pen-y-ghent (2273 feet) one of the most impressive summits of the Way and a fine viewpoint. Beyond it the path descends past Hunt Pot to the village of Horton in Ribblesdale. Old drove roads and a Roman road are followed in part now as the Way leaves the head of Ribblesdale by Cam End and runs along the ridge between Widdale and Sleddale to drop into the broad, green expanse of Wensleydale at Hawes. Some 100,000 sheep a year are marketed in this compact little town.

The Pennine Way climbs out of Wensleydale not far from the famous waterfall of Hardraw Force to reach the summit of Great Shunner Fell (2340 feet) and then curves east to the little village of Thwaite in Swaledale, where the road comes through the Buttertubs Pass joining the two dales. It now follows the steep side of Swaledale to cross the river not far from Keld and climb over Stonesdale Moor to Tan Hill. The pub here is, at 1732 feet, the highest in England. From Swaledale to Teesdale is a considerable day's tramp across the expanse of Stainmore and there is an alternative loop to the Way to take one eastward into the small town of Bowes on the Roman road that here crosses the Pennines. The main line of the path crosses the River Greta by the fine natural arch of God's Bridge, and the two paths meet again at the head of Blackton Reservoir.

From Middleton in Teesdale the Way follows the Yorkshire bank of the Tees to High Force. This famous fall is now assured of a regular force of water by the construction of the controversial reservoir at Cow Green some miles upstream. The Way passes not far from the dam and close to another cascade at Caldron Snout, where, as at High Force, the Tees crosses the dark resistant rock band of the Whin Sill. This rock is also responsible for the next important feature on the route and one of the most dramatic in its whole length. After crossing a desolate tract of moorland, following the banks

The impressive outline of Pen-y-ghent from Churn Milk Hole. The Way climbs to the summit of the fell.

of Maize Beck, the Way comes suddenly to a giant amphitheatre where the ground drops away at the foot of dark cliffs of Whin Sill basalt. This is High Cup Nick, and the path skirts the northern cliffs, descending gradually to the pleasant village of Dufton, built round a spacious green. Below lies the Vale of Eden with its rich green fields and warm red earth making an abrupt contrast with the Pennine slopes; the dividing line between the two is in fact a vast fault or earth fracture which has dropped the rocks to the west by thousands of feet.

Now begins the long ascent over Knock Fell, Great and Little Dun Fells and past Tees Head to Cross Fell (2930 feet), the highest point on the Pennines and on the Way. The flat crest of Cross Fell is a prominent land-mark from the hills of the Lake District, and on a good day is itself an un-paralleled viewpoint from which the hills of Galloway, over the Border, and in the north The Cheviot, at the far end of the Way, can be seen. From the level top of the fell the Way drops 400 feet to meet the old track coming up from Kirkland to Garrigill, and follows it eastwards past old mine workings to drop down into the valley of the South Tyne.

A little farther up the valley is the market town of Alston, said to be the highest in England. It is perched on a steep hill above the river, over which there is a stone bridge crossed by the Pennine Way. About $2\frac{1}{2}$ miles north-west of Alston are the remains of a Roman fort at Whitley Castle, and here the Way joins the line of a Roman road, Maiden Way, which it follows for some miles along the west side of the South Tyne valley. The next section of the Way is dominated by the most famous of all the works of the Romans—the Wall.

The Pennine Way meets the Wall just after crossing the A69 Newcastle–Carlisle west of Greenhead and follows it through its most impressive section, passing several forts, turrets and milecastles. Over Winshields, Peel Crag, above Crag Lough to Hotbank Crags the Wall clings to the top of the natural boundary formed by the hard Whin Sill, which makes a kind of steep escarpment. Just before Housesteads, one of the best preserved forts on the Wall, the Way starts out northwards again between Greenlee and Broomlee Loughs. For nearly all the rest of its length it remains in or on the boundary of the Northumberland National Park (see p. 79).

Passing through the plantations of the Forestry Commission's Wark Forest, the path crosses the Wark Burn and climbs over Shitlington Crags to drop down to the North Tyne valley at Bellingham. The town suffered badly from a fire in 1780, but lying as it does on one of the ancient raiding routes from Scotland it had probably been subject to similar disasters earlier. Con-tinuing northwards the Way follows the east bank of the Hareshaw Burn, keeping to the high ground, over Lord's Shaw and Brownrigg Head and through more forests to Redesdale, another raiders' route. From here it climbs over the hills around the head of the Coquet, passing the notable Roman camps at Chew Green and crossing the Border for the first time. The Way now follows the Border and the edge of the national park over Beefstand Hill and Mazie Law to Windy Gyle (2034 feet). Just beyond here the old drove road of Clennell Street crosses the Way, providing escape routes north to Bowmont Water and south to Uswayford and Alwinton.

A spur of the Pennine Way takes one from the main path just before Auchope Cairn onto the broad plateau of The Cheviot (2676 feet). Then, keeping close to the Border fence, the path skirts the deep cleft of Hen Hole, climbs to The Schill (1985 feet) and follows a ridge route past the head of the Halter Burn and down its valley branching off to the little village of Kirk Yetholm.

The Pennine Way provides some of the roughest walking to be found in Britain. It certainly should not be attempted by anyone unable to steer a course by map and compass in bad visibility. In good weather most people could probably manage up to fifteen miles of hill walking, but boggy ground, the brutal tussocky moor grass, or rough heather, can cut this down on the Pennines. In rain, mist, snow or high winds the Way can provide exhausting and even dangerous exposure conditions for the hardiest walkers. There are a number of books to guide one along the Way, but the most compact is that by Tom Stephenson, which includes map sections while still fitting an anorak pocket easily.

Ridgeway

One of the long-standing ideas for a national long-distance path has been a chalkland route running from a point near Cambridge right down to the coast of Devon near Seaton. In 1972 the Secretary of State for the Environment approved a line of eighty-four and a half miles forming the central portion of this route and stretching from Ivinghoe Beacon in Buckinghamshire to Overton Hill near Avebury in Wiltshire. The Chilterns section, from Ivinghoe to Goring on the Thames, is planned as a footpath and is, at forty-four and a half miles, just the longer. Over the remaining forty miles from Streatley to Overton Hill the route will be a bridleway and can be used by those on horse or cycle as well as by walkers.

From Ivinghoe Beacon, the first of several hills of over 800 feet along the route, the Ridgeway holds to the ridge of the Chilterns, passing above the

Ivinghoe Beacon, at present the north-eastern end of the Ridgeway path, which follows the line of the Chilterns, overlooking the Vale of Aylesbury.

now-restored windmill at Pitstone and crossing the Tring and Wendover gaps through the escarpment. But from Chinnor onwards through the Oxfordshire section the path descends to the foot of the scarp, following the ancient Icknield Way for some twelve miles. It crosses the A40 just at the foot of the famous winding ascent engineered by Telford and just beyond which a massive cutting is planned to carry the M40 and today's less tolerant traffic. Reaching the Thames just below Wallingford, the path follows the eastern bank down river to Goring, where it crosses into Berkshire.

For most of its line so far the path has been within the boundaries of the Chilterns area of outstanding natural beauty; now it enters and remains within the North Wessex Downs area. From Streatley the path ascends to follow the Ridgeway proper, the ancient trackway used from time immemorial by travellers along the Berkshire Downs. Something of its history is reflected in the many sites of archaeological interest lying along the route. The site of the battle of Ashdown, just over 1100 years ago, lies some two and a half miles west of Streatley; here the Danes suffered their first major defeat and the foundations of King Alfred's Wessex were laid. Passing an even older fortification at Segsbury, south of Wantage, the Ridgeway follows the curve of the downs round to Whitehorse Hill and Uffington Castle, another earthwork, and past Wayland's Smithy at Ashbury, just before crossing into Wiltshire. Still following the old trackway, the path then curves south past Liddington Castle and west to Barbury Castle on Marlborough Downs. Hackpen Hill, at nearly 900 feet, is one of the highest points on the route, and the Ridgeway traces its length before dropping southwards towards the Kennet Valley and the A4. Here one is no great distance from Silbury Hill, Avebury and the wealth of ancient sites in this part of Wiltshire.

South Downs Way

The country's first long-distance bridleway, the South Downs Way was opened in 1972. Some 800 people gathered at Beachy Head for the ceremony, at which riders and cyclists as well as walkers were represented. Since the Countryside Act of 1968 cyclists have had the right to use bridleways, though in narrow or obstructed places they should give way to walkers or riders. Beachy Head is the starting point of a footpath-only section which follows the cliffs to Cuckmere Haven, but riders and cyclists start on the bridleway from the same side of Eastbourne and no great distance from Beachy Head.

The South Downs Way runs for some eighty miles between Eastbourne and the Hampshire border following the high land of the South Downs. Since it keeps to the north-facing scarp of the Downs it is well inland from the line of resorts and dormitory towns. All of the route lies within the Sussex Downs area of outstanding natural beauty. Eventually it is hoped that the Way will be extended westwards from the Hampshire border along the line of chalk hills that stretches to Winchester.

From the outskirts of Eastbourne the bridleway follows the high edge of the Downs round the west of the town as far as Willingdon Hill. It then turns north-westward across the Downs to the village of Jevington. Beyond lies Windover Hill, one of the finest viewpoints on the Way, and at its foot is the famous Long Man of Wilmington, an enormous figure carved in the chalk of the hillside. At Alfriston, in the Cuckmere Valley, the bridleway is joined by the footpath loop from Beachy Head which traverses the cliffs of the Seven Sisters to Cuckmere Haven and then comes up the side of the valley by way of Westdean and Litlington. This loop is not at all suitable for horses or cycles and is for walkers only. In several places cliff falls are a danger, and at Birling Gap a short diversion had to be made.

From Alfriston the Way sets out over Firle Beacon to the Ouse valley, crossing the river at Southease. The Beacon (713 feet) is another good viewpoint. Lewes lies just to the north, and the Way makes a broad sweep to the south and west of the town, crossing the Lewes–Brighton road at the Newmarket Inn. It then turns westwards again over a third outstanding viewpoint, Ditchling Beacon, and reaches the Brighton Road at Pyecombe. The Devil's Dyke, a popular drive out from Brighton, is on the line of the Way as it continues to Edburton Hill, where it crosses the boundary from East to West Sussex. Below lies the valley of the River Adur, and the Way descends

The view from Devil's Dyke looking along the line of the Way westwards to Chanctonbury Ring.

from Beeding Hill and through Bramber to cross the river by a new bridle-way bridge. Keeping to the scarp above Wiston Park, the Way reaches Chanctonbury Ring, another of the well visited parts of the Downs.

Just south of the village of Washington the Way crosses the Worthing road, and then starts out over a succession of hills—Highden, Barnsfarm, Sullington, Kithurst and Rackham—onto Amberley Mount overlooking the valley of the Arun. It crosses the river at Houghton and climbs again to Bury, Westburton and Bignor Hills. Above Bignor, where there are well pre-served remains of a Roman Villa, the Roman road of Stane Street strikes straight across the Downs towards Chichester. Here the Way swings north-west towards Woolavington Down and enters a more wooded section of the Downs scarp before dropping down to the Chichester road just south of Cocking. Cocking Down is another fine viewpoint on the Way, which now goes over Linch Down and Didling Hill past the Devil's Jumps. By Buriton Farm it starts to climb again, passing just south of Beacon Hill (793 feet), the site of a hill fort. Over Harting Downs to Tower Hill at the northern end of the Uppark Estate, the Way crosses the steep roads down to South Harting and follows Forty Acre Lane as far as the West Sussex county boundary with Hampshire.

The official end of the Way is by Sunwood Farm, about a mile east of Buriton, but the bridleway continues into Hampshire and across the Ports-mouth Road to the Butser Hill country park. An extension westward as far as Winchester is now planned.

South-West Peninsula Coast Path

It was an early plan of the National Parks Commission to create a path that would offer continuous cliff-top walking on the Cornish coast. In their second annual report (1951) the Commission went further, expressing the hope 'ultimately to have a path round the coast of the peninsula from a suit-able point in Somerset to a point in Dorset'. While this has not yet become a reality, five sections of a 515-mile coast path were approved at various dates between 1952 and 1963, and it is now possible to walk over a good deal of the route. Within its length it includes much of the grandest coastal scenery in these islands: rugged cliffs, wide bays and beaches, sand dunes and pebble ridges, beautiful inlets and estuaries. It also includes some of the most popular holiday coasts, so that while the path has its wild and romantic stretches it is never too remote from the resorts, small ports and villages of the south-west. For many it will be a path walked only in short lengths on the cliffs that lie around a chosen holiday place, though with the knowledge that the walk could be extended in either direction as far as one's legs or one's holiday would last. Others may tackle the whole length, in sections, over a number of holidays. Certainly there is enough interest on this path to make a year seem too short to walk it in.

The path is described here in the five sections: Somerset and North Devon, North Cornwall, South Cornwall, South Devon, and Dorset, working round from Minehead to Studland.

SOMERSET AND NORTH DEVON COAST PATH (82 MILES)

Starting at the pleasant Somerset resort of Minehead, with its fine quay built in 1616 to initiate nearly three centuries of prosperous trading for the port, the first part of the path follows the steep coast of the Exmoor National Park. It leaves Minehead from a point just by the harbour, at the end of the quay, and climbs via Culver Cliff to North Hill, a wide plateau criss-crossed by tracks, making for the viewpoint of Selworthy Beacon. A mile beyond the Beacon the path forks to provide the first of a number of optional detours, this one to Hurtstone Point. Descending through Bossington to the broad sweep of Porlock Bay, the path then follows the line of the beach to Porlock Weir, where it climbs again, by the edge of Yearnor Wood, to continue through Culbone, noted for its tiny church only twelve yards long by twelve feet wide. Beyond Silcombe, Broomstreet and Yenworthy to the Devon boundary

233

at County Gate, where it meets the A39 coast road, the way proceeds to-wards Countisbury, where there is again an alternative path out to Foreland Point, and then on to Lynmouth.

Generally speaking the walker picks his own way through towns, villages and resorts on this long-distance path; here he may choose to take the cliff railway up to Lynton to rejoin the coast path at North Walk. Passing the Valley of the Rocks, and above another beauty spot at Woody Bay, it now follows an old coach road to Hunter's Inn, near the dramatic cleave of Heddon's Mouth. The way on to Combe Martin lies across Trentishoe Down, bending inland to cross Sherrycombe Water, and over Great and Little Hangman. From here to Ilfracombe the path coincides from time to time with the coast road, through Watermouth (nineteenth-century Gothic castle) and Hele. Here again the path is picked up at Torrs Walk on the other side of the resort, whence it continues past Lee Bay, closely following the coast round Bull Point and Morte Point to Woolacombe. Keeping to the seaward side of the downs, and over Baggy Point, it reaches Croyde Bay and Saunton Sands, and then over Swanpool Bridge into Braunton.

At Braunton there is another break in the path, which is picked up again at Westward Ho!, reached by bus through Barnstaple and Bideford or by way of the Instow–Appledore ferry. From here there is a cliff-top path to Buck's Mills and a fine approach to Clovelly along the wooded Hobby Drive. The path now makes for Hartland Point with its steeply dipping rocks like tiles stacked on edge, and, still following the cliff top along the rugged Atlantic coast of the Hartland Peninsula, reaches the boundary of Cornwall at Marsland Mouth.

CORNWALL NORTH COAST PATH (135 MILES)

From the Devon county boundary the path sets out along the cliffs and into Cornwall, past the village of Morwenstow, home of the poet R. S. Hawker, and on by Steeple Point to Bude. The chief resort of North Cornwall, Bude enjoys popularity with surfers as well as family holidaymakers. Crossing Bude's canal, one can take up the path again at Compass Point and follow the coast past Widemouth Sands to climb over Dizzard Point and some fine cliffs to Crackington Haven; here and at Millook Haven are spectacular examples of sharp folding in the rocks. Beeny Cliff, on the next stretch to Boscastle, is the subject of a poem by Hardy, who worked as a young man on the church of St Juliot nearby. Boscastle, with its picturesque, rock-guarded harbour tucked into the drowned valley of the Valency, ushers in an unfor-gettable four miles to Tintagel over some of the best cliff scenery on the path. King Arthur's Castle crowns Tintagel Head, and whether or not you believe the legends it must certainly have been a strong defensive site over a long enough period of history. By Trebarwith Strand and Tregardock Cliff, the path continues to Port Isaac, a splendid unspoiled fishing village, then is diverted a little way inland to Portquin before rounding Pentire Head to Hayle Bay and Polzeath.

There is a ferry across the River Camel to Padstow (famous for its Hobby Horse Dance and May celebrations) from a point just below Cassock Hill. The path then follows the western side of the estuary to Stepper Point, continuing down the coast past the oddly named Pepper Hole and Butter Hole to Harlyn Bay. After the curve of Mother Ivey's Bay, it then rounds Trevose Head to the sands of Constantine Bay and Treyarnon Beach, passing Porth-cothan Beach and Park Head on the way to Bedruthan Steps, a fine and justly popular stretch of rocky coastline. Between here and Newquay the path drops down to Mawgan Porth and then follows the cliffs along Water-gate Bay. In May 1973 a ceremony on the cliffs at the edge of Newquay marked the official opening of the 268 miles of the Cornwall Coast Path.

Newquay is the largest resort in Cornwall. It has a collection of attractive beaches, and is a centre for surf riding; in Fistral Bay the surfers come in on 9-foot Malibu boards. After crossing the River Gannel west of Newquay the path follows a stretch of dune coast to Perranporth, then more cliffs around St Agnes Head, and through Portreath to some fine walking on Carvannel and

Walkers on the North Cornwall Coast Path at Clodgy Point near St Ives.

Reskajeage Downs out to Godrevy Point with its island and lighthouse. Over Gwithian Bridge and another stretch of dunes, the River Hayle is reached, and can be crossed by a ferry, if in operation, or by turning south into Hayle where there is a bridge. St Ives is the next major settlement, a maze of narrow streets and cobbled passageways with as many resident artists and potters as fishermen. It is the prelude to a long stretch of particularly fine and rugged coastline, past Zennor and Gurnard's Head and out to Cape Cornwall. The cliffs offer some of Cornwall's best climbing, which may be seen from above by walkers on the path, though others may prefer to turn their attention inland to the logans, quoits and other monuments to the earliest inhabitants of this peninsula of West Penwith. From Cape Cornwall the path strikes south to Sennen Cove, still a working fishing port, and out to the granite pillars of Land's End, where, as Defoe says, Nature ended her account when she meted out the island. The last stretch of the path goes out to Gwennap Head, and past Porthcurno and the open-air theatre of Minack to Lamorna Cove, with its pleasantly sheltered valley behind. After the attractive fishing village of Mousehole, it joins the coast road into Penzance.

CORNWALL SOUTH COAST PATH (133 MILES)

'A place of good business, well built and populous' was Defoe's description of Penzance. Besides being the terminus of the railway and the departure point for the Scilly Isles, the town is the starting point of the South Cornwall Path, which sets out eastwards along Mount's Bay from the Albert pier towards Marazion and the granite hump of St Michael's Mount, reached by low-tide causeway from the shore. The path follows the sands on the eastern side of the bay past Perranuthnoe, Prussia Cove and the gleaming Prah Sands to Porthleven, and then crosses the narrow Loe Bar which separates a two-mile fresh-water lake from the sea. Continuing by way of Gunwalloe Cove, Poldhu Cove and Mullion Cove, past the monument to Marconi, the path mounts the spectacular serpentine cliffs of the Lizard Peninsula, which are well seen at Kynance Cove, one of the high spots of the whole path. The Lizard is the most southerly point of the British mainland and a landmark to ships entering and leaving the Channel. Here the path turns north along the eastern coast of the peninsula to Cadgwith and by way of Kennack Sands and Black Head to Coverack, a fine unspoilt working port. North of Coverack the cliffs have been extensively quarried, and the path has to deviate inland near Manacle Point to Rosenithon, returning to the coast at the little harbour of Porthoustock. Another inland diversion follows, through Trenance, but the path joins the coast again at Porthallow and follows it to Gillan Harbour (fordable at low tide), Dennis Head and St Anthony-in-Meneage. The next part of the path, at Mawnan, here faces one across the wide and beautiful Helford River, and it is necessary to follow the southern bank of the river inland to Helford, where there is a ferry. Resuming its line northwards, over Rosemullion Head, the path then rounds Pennance Point and enters Falmouth by Swanpool Beach, continuing along the coast to Pendennis Head, where the famous Tudor fortress faces that of St Mawes across the mouth of the fine deep-water haven of Carrick Roads.

There is a ferry from the old town of Falmouth to St Mawes on the east side of the Roads, and another across the Porthcuel River to St Anthony-in-Roseland, where the path resumes, following the coast closely round St Anthony Head, Gerrans Bay and Nare Head to the fishing village of Portloe. Across Veryan Bay can be seen the Dodman, another familiar land-mark to sailors. This massive, rocky headland is crowned by a tall stone tower, and the remains can also be seen of a promontory fort. The path continues from the Point around Gorran Haven and into Mevagissey, a pic-turesque fishing village and harbour, popular with artists. North of Meva-gissey the line is behind Black Head to Porthpean on the wide St Austell Bay. Inland one can catch a glimpse here of the characteristic white china clay tips, and away round the bay is the little port of Par, from which is shipped much of the product of this prosperous mining industry. The path con-tinues by way of Par Sands to Polmear and Polkerris, where it climbs again to a fine stretch of cliffs around Gribbin Head to the outskirts of Fowey.

Fowey is full of history; in the time of Edward III it furnished more war-ships for the king than any other port, and was so powerful it put the Cinque Ports right out of countenance. A ferry crosses Fowey River to Polruan and to another fine stretch of cliff scenery, along Lantic Bay and Lantivet Bay to Polperro, one of the best known of Cornish fishing villages and harbours, and on around Talland and Portnadler Bays to Looe. West Looe and East Looe are joined by a bridge; the path threads its way through the narrow streets of the little town, and out through Downderry and Portwrinkle to the long curve of Whitesand Bay stretching round to Rame Head, making a small diversion inland to avoid rifle ranges on Blarrick Cliff. It then turns round Penlee Point, through the villages of Cawsand and Kingsand, before bending inland by Mount Edgcumbe Park to reach the Tamar Estuary and the ferry for Plymouth at Cremyll.

DEVON SOUTH COAST PATH (93 MILES)

The city of Plymouth stands in the arms of the 'Y' formed by the drowned river mouths of the Tamar (Hamoaze) and the Plym (Cattewater) which join as Plymouth Sound. The famous Hoe is a limestone outcrop facing straight down the Sound, and providing a magnificent viewpoint. The next stretch of the coast path starts at Turnchapel, across the Cattewater from the main part of the city, skirts the west side of Stamford Fort and climbs Staddon Heights, with fine views back over the Sound, continuing southward to Wembury Point and then east round Wembury Bay to the estuary of the Yealm. This river mouth, the first of several on this section of the path, can normally be crossed by ferry; the alternative inland detour would be at least five miles extra. The path continues along the coast, but making a small inland detour at Mothecombe to reach a point on the Erme estuary fordable on a low and falling tide; again the road crossing is two miles upstream. The next river, the Avon, beyond the little resort of Bigbury with its 'sea trams' out to Burgh Island, can also be waded by the hardy, but there is an occasional ferry over to Bantham. The path then goes on by the links of Thurlestone, round the attractive Hope Cove, and out to the headland of Bolt Tail. There follows a splendid cliff walk, over National Trust land, to Bolt Head, crossing Bolberry Down and the Warren, before the path turns northwards to descend into the wooded slopes of Salcombe Harbour. The ferry crosses this estuary from the Harbour to East Portlemouth, and the path now traverses a long stretch of open cliff to Gammon Head and Prawle Point, the southernmost tip of Devon. Here and at Lannacombe the raised beach is prominent, the line of the former cliffs appearing just inland from the path. Start Point, to which the path now climbs, is formed from the hardened and contorted rocks known as schists; in them can be seen the gleam of mica.

From Start Point the path turns northwards along the curve of Start Bay to Torcross and Slapton Ley. Here it follows the pebble ridge between the Ley and the sea as far as Strete Gate, where the old coach road goes up the hill into Strete, and then returns to the coast and the delightful Blackpool Sands, before rounding Blackstone Point into the estuary of the Dart by Dartmouth Castle. There are frequent ferries from the ancient and historic port over the Dart to Kingswear, where the path retraces its course down the eastern side of the estuary, skirting some woodland and making a short inland detour at Coleton, before reaching the coast again, which it follows to Berry Head. Here there is a country park of just over 100 acres, with fine views over Tor Bay, interesting fortifications, and a seabird colony on the cliffs. The path now descends to the fishing port of Brixham, with its fine harbour where, in 1688, William of Orange landed on his way to become William III of England. Beyond the town, skirting the golf course to reach Elbury Cove, the path continues as far as the edge of Paignton, where it breaks off, resuming at the other end of the built-up area of Torquay.

From Hope's Nose, near Torquay, the footpath follows Babbacombe Bay to strike out over the red cliffs that characterise the whole of the next stretch of the path as far as Budleigh Salterton, which lies beyond the Exe. The Teign is crossed by a ferry not far from its mouth, to the resort of Teignmouth, but beyond here the railway follows the coast so closely that there is no room for an adequate path. Just inland from the railway, a path north of Dawlish goes out to Dawlish Warren, curving around the mouth of the Exe. To cross this broad estuary, it is necessary to turn back inland to Starcross, where there is a ferry to Exmouth.

The path picks up again just east of this town and, passing behind the Services ranges at Straight Point, sets out over the impressive red cliffs known as The Floors to Budleigh Salterton. The River Otter is crossed by a foot-bridge a short distance inland, and the path then returns to the coast, follow-ing the cliffs to Ladram Bay. From here it climbs to nearly 500 feet at High Peak, the finest red cliff of them all, before descending to the valley of the Sid and the pleasant resort of Sidmouth. Now begins a switchback section of cliff walking, over Salcombe Hill, Dunscombe Cliff and Coxe's Cliff, 500-foot heights separated by deep combes, to Branscombe Mouth. The red of the cliffs has now given way to white as the path climbs over South Down Common to reach Beer Head, a 400-foot wall of chalk. The village of Beer merges into the resort of Seaton, east of which is a coastline dominated by the Great Landslip. For nearly six miles the path makes its way along the under-cliff, a rugged terrain part of which is a national nature reserve, to cross the Dorset boundary just short of Lyme Regis.

DORSET COAST PATH (72 MILES)

The historic port of Lyme Regis, with its curved stone breakwater known as the Cobb, its bow-fronted Georgian houses and its precipitous streets, stands in a combe facing the wide bay to which it gives its name. The path sets out up Timber Hill to the east of the town, keeping back from the treacherous edge of Black Ven, which, like the cliffs on the other side of Lyme, is subject to landslips and has already accounted for the coast road. It then descends to the Charmouth gap, crosses the footbridge near the mouth of the Char, and begins the next climb, this time to Golden Cap, at 618 feet the highest point on the South coast and a fine viewpoint. The name comes from the yellow sands which, capped by a chert bed, form the upper part of the impressive cliff. From here the line of the path ahead to the east can be seen as a succes-sion of only slightly lower summits. In the dip immediately below is the tiny settlement of Seatown, followed by Doghouse Hill and Thorncombe Beacon, then another dip to Eype Mouth, and a climb over West Cliff and down to West Bay, the seaside and harbour of the town of Bridport, which lies one mile inland. The path now takes to the top of East Cliff, another stretch of golden-yellow cliff, skirting the golf course, and dropping to the River Bride and the village of Burton Bradstock.

Some three miles east of Burton, at Bexington, alternative routes are pre-sented to the walker. He can either take an inland path climbing the ridge of

Wears Hill and continuing along the edge of the downs, or he can turn from the beginning of Chesil Beach into the village of Abbotsbury and follow a path along the shores of the Fleet, the lagoon which separates the Beach from the mainland. The first of these choices keeps the magnificent views, passing the gigantic candlestick of the Hardy monument at its highest point and returning to the coast at Osmington Mills, east of Weymouth. The second, keeping closer to the sea, will be the obvious choice of those wishing to visit or stop in Abbotsbury or Weymouth. Those who would set out along the beach towards Portland are warned: it is over twelve miles to Chesil and shingle all the way.

The Dorset Coast Path winding over the chalk cliffs near Durdle Door.

Beyond Weymouth the coastal loop of path restarts by Overcombe, where the coast road bends inland, and continues along the cliffs by Redcliff Point and Black Head to Osmington Mills. Here it is joined by the inland route, which comes down from White Horse Hill and through Osmington. Some spectacular cliff scenery opens out along the next stretch, past Ringstead Bay, the 500-foot chalk headland of White Nothe, Bat's Head and the natural arch of Durdle Door, to the perfect symmetry of Lulworth Cove. There is now a gap in the path, for the next six miles or so to Kimmeridge Bay are occupied by the Services as part of an extensive artillery range—so extensive, in fact, that when firing is in progress an inland detour of nearly fifteen miles must be made to regain the coast. At certain times, however, the road along the crest of the Purbeck Hills can be used, descending through Steeple and Kimmeridge to the sea again. From Kimmeridge Bay the path goes along the cliffs of dark blue-black bituminous shale (once burnt for oil) above the Ledges, climbs over the 500-foot dome of Hounstout Cliff to the dark waters of Chapman's Pool, and swings south to St Alban's Head, where there is a small, fortress-like Norman chapel. Between here and Durlston Head are Dancing Ledge, an impressive platform of rock just below high water mark, and Tilly Whim Caves. The path is broken by the pleasant resort of Swanage, and starts out on its last stretch halfway up Swanage Bay to climb Ballard Down and strike out to the Foreland, overlooking the Old Harry Rocks. It then descends to Studland and follows the sand dunes round Studland Bay to the entrance of Poole Harbour, where it ends at the ferry from South Haven Point to Sandbanks.

Short General Reading List

Britain's National Parks, ed. H. Abrahams. Country Life, 1959

Britain's Structure and Scenery, L. Dudley Stamp. Collins 'New Naturalist' Series; and Fontana, 1960

The Coastline of England and Wales, J. A. Steers. Cambridge University Press, 1964

Mountains and Moorlands, W. H. Pearsall. Collins 'New Naturalist' Series; and Fontana, revised edn 1972

National Parks, a tourist's guide, R. H. A. Staniforth. Dalesman, 1971

Geology and Scenery in England and Wales, A. E. Trueman. Penguin, 1961

Rural Rides, William Cobbett, 1830; edited by George Woodcock for Penguin, 1967

A Tour through the whole Island of Great Britain, Daniel Defoe, 1724–6; Dent, Everyman's Library, revised edn 1962

Additional Reading

ON NATIONAL PARKS AND LONG-DISTANCE FOOTPATHS

Brecon Beacons National Park, HMSO Guide, ed. Margaret Davies. 1967

Dartmoor, L. A. Harvey and D. St Leger Gordon. Collins 'New Naturalist' Series, 1953

Dartmoor, Guide to, William Crossing, 1909. Reprinted, David and Charles, 1970

Dartmoor National Park, HMSO Guide, ed. W. G. Hoskins. Revised 1972

Exmoor National Park, HMSO Guide, ed. John Coleman-Cooke. 1970

Roof of England, A. H. Griffin. Hale, 1970

Portrait of the Lakes, Norman Nicholson. Hale, 1963

Greater Lakeland, Norman Nicholson. Hale, 1969

Lake District National Park, HMSO Guide, ed. W. H. Pearsall. Revised 1969

Northumberland National Park Handbook, Northumberland County Council, 1969

Northumberland National Park, HMSO Guide, ed. John Philipson. 1969

North York Moors National Park, HMSO Guide, ed. Arthur Raistrick. Revised 1971

The Peak District, K. C. Edwards. Collins 'New Naturalist' Series, 1962

Peak District National Park, HMSO Guide, ed. Patrick Monkhouse. Revised 1971

Pembrokeshire Coast National Park, HMSO Guide, ed. Dillwyn Miles. 1973

Shell Guide to South-West Wales, Vyvyan Rees. Faber, 1969

Snowdonia National Park, W. M. Condry. Collins 'New Naturalist' Series; and Fontana, 1969

Snowdonia National Park, Snowdonia Park Joint Advisory Committee, 1969 and 1970

Snowdonia National Park, HMSO Guide, ed. Edmund Vale. Revised 1973

The Yorkshire Dales, M. Hartley and J. Ingilby. Dent, 1963

The Pennine Dales, Arthur Raistrick. Eyre and Spottiswoode, 1968

Yorkshire Dales National Park, HMSO Guide, ed. I. G. Simmons. 1971

The Cleveland Way, W. Cowley. Dalesman, 1969

The Cleveland Way, A. Falconer. HMSO, 1972

The Shell Book of Offa's Dyke Path, Frank Noble. Queen Anne Press. Revised 1972

The Pembrokeshire Coast Path, John Barrett. HMSO, 1973

The Pennine Way, Tom Stephenson. HMSO, 1970

A Pennine Way Companion, A. Wainwright. 1968

The Shell Book of the Pennine Way, Michael Marriott. Queen Anne Press, 1969

The South West Coast Path, Edward Pyatt. David and Charles, 1971

The Shell Book of the South West Coast Path, S. F. Marriott. Queen Anne Press, 1970

Index